INSIDE THE I[
WORDS OF

Published By

Prisoners Writes Publishing (PWP)

ISBN 978-0-9863888-0-4

Manufactured in the United States of America

$19.99
ISBN 978-0-9863888-0-4
51999>

9 780986 388804

Thank you for your Support
I am sure that you'll find
the contents of this book
thought provoking and very
useful. Peace & Blessings
Sincerely, Master Djhuti Mansa Musa Menes
"The Struggle Continues"

This book needs no introduction, only a dedication and a few acknowledgments. This book is dedicated to my mother, CECELIA McEACHIN. You are the reason I breathe and without you I would not exist, nor would my beautiful sisters, my wonderful children, or all of my nieces and nephews who I love dearly.

My mom told me that she was inspired by what I wrote to her in my letters and that she wanted to edit my letters into a one or two page thought, which she felt could be beneficial to those interested in what is on the Mind of those of us Inside Prison.

My mother started working on this book, "INSIDE THE INSIDES MIND" through letters that I was mailing her until she fell ill and was unable to put it out. Once she fell ill, the individuals that she was working with to put the book out kept all of the material she had gathered from my letters to her. Then her home was mysteriously burned down and numerous important documents of both mine and hers were destroyed in the fire. I am just glad that my Mom is still alive.

ii

[Note: At this writing, Cecelia McEachin was physically alive, but she has since passed as is outlined in the dedication which is a Eulogy that was done at the send-off.]

And I want her to know that it is her will being done. And since you taught me how to fight mother, I have also dedicated a section of this book to doing just that: Fighting Back!

I must also acknowledge my aunt/ mother Frances McEachin Collins. I love you dearly, and although I am your nephew, in reality I am also your son, and your daughters are my sisters and their children are my children.

I must also acknowledge my dad, Earl Edelin, you taught me how to think and act like a man. You encouraged me to get an education and you taught me about business and corporations. But what stood out the most is when you explained to me your perception of the Big Bang Theory and how the universe was created. That one conversation was one the most important catalyst for my continued search for knowledge. You said to me, "Son, you are the Universe", If you start there, although your journey for knowledge will never end, your foundation will be able to hold the weight of your knowledge, because the Universe is infinite."

There is a host of friends, relatives and comrades who I will acknowledge without naming because there is absolutely too many of you and I don't want to offend anyone because I missed your name. Just know who you are and know that I love and acknowledge you all, especially those of you who feel the struggle. Much respect to my brother-in-law, who has been a part of the family forever and have always stepped up. And of course there is a special Lady, Cleopatra Essence, who outside of my immediate family, has shown me through deeds that you're more than worthy of my heart. The time did not break you, and you're standing firm in the struggle. I love you dearly. You and the special ladies whom I named the Sugar Hill Gang after my favorite rap group. To Brother Abdul R. Mahdi, Brother Anthony Muhammad of Mosque #4, and Brother Dyrell Muhammad, aka Brother D, much love, honor and respect. Last but not least, I give special honors to all of my comrades, and all of my Homies, that are stand up men who are prisoners of war locked down in The Belly of the Beast.

"INSIDE THE INSIDES MIND" (WORD OF THE WEEK)

Dedicated to Mother, Cecelia McEachin: Her Eulogy

"CECELIA McEACHIN, MY BEST FRIEND"

The woman that lay before you today, my mother, Cecelia McEachin is no ordinary woman. Because ordinary women produce ordinary children. Cecelia McEachin has produced extraordinary children, grandchildren and great-grandchildren, and she has extraordinary nieces and nephews. She has extraordinary Brothers and Sisters, aunts and uncles and extended family and friends, some of you are here today to pay your respects, and others are not physically present, but are here in spirit to pay homage to the great woman that lay before you. The fact that you all are here is a testament to how extraordinary Cecelia McEachin truly is. Yes, I said Cecelia McEachin is an extraordinary woman. I will not speak of my mother as if she is no longer here. To do that would be to deny my very existence, and the existence of those who have descended from the womb of this Magnificent Black Woman. I would be denying the existence of my sisters, the existence of my children, the existence of my nieces and nephews. Within our genetic and spiritual make up, and within the genetic makeup of her Brothers; Lawrence, Gregory, Jerome, Bengiman, Anthony, and Antonio; and within the genetic and spiritual make up of her sisters, Rosetta and Frances, and all of their descendants, Cecelia McEachin exist and will continue to live. In that sense, she is not dead:

In the Holy Bible; John 5:24-25 Jesus said:

"Most assuredly I say to you, he who hears my word and believes in him who has sent me has everlasting life, and shall not come into judgment, but has passed from death into life. Most assuredly, I say to you, the hour is coming, and now is, when the dead will hear the voice of the Son of God, and those who hear will live."

My mother not only heard the voice of the Son of God. She took heed to the message that was conveyed to her by the Son of God, and sat that message on the Seat of her Soul and made that message a part of her. And therefore she became a true Christian. And what is a true Christian? A true Christian is one who has been crystallized into oneness with God through the examples of Jesus the Christ.

"THE WORDS OF A SPECIAL MOTHER"

My mother would often say to me; "Son, you're an Angel; you're a gift from God to the World". She said it so much that I started to believing it. And when you believe that you're an Angel, and you know that Angels do God's will, it is your duty to do God's work without deviating or second guessing the mission that you have been ordained by God to carry out. My mother was and is constantly teaching me to be pure in heart. To teach a Man to be pure in heart, you must yourself be pure in heart, in word and in deed. And this she is.

So I say to you all today who are gathered here, "Cecelia McEachin lives". You can rest assure that she is literally within us, physically and spiritually. And you can rest assure that she is with God.

In the Aquarian Gospel, it is written that: "Death is no enemy to man, it is a friend who, when the works of life is done, just cuts the cords that binds the human boat to earth, that it may sail on smoother seas. No language can describe a mother's worth, and yours was tried and true. But she was not called hence until her task was done. Let your mother rest in peace. Just let her noble life be strength and inspiration unto you".

"MEMORIES OF MOTHER"

The fond memories that we have of this extraordinary Magnificent Black woman that lay before us will forever be etched in our minds. Lets us take a moment to learn from her. First, know that my mother loves continually and unconditionally. She has never denied anyone anything ever asked of her that she was capable of doing. She would go out of her way, often making sacrifices that she really couldn't afford to make just to see you happy and put a smile on your face was her reward.

I knew that she had learned that lesson from her mother, my grandmother, Rosa Lee McEachin, who was, and is, one of the most graceful, loving and giving woman to have ever walked the face of this earth. And we all know that grandmother never denied any of us anything that she was capable of doing for us. And I am proud to say that was one of the many valuable lessons that I learned from my mother. And it is because of her love that I have saved, educated, rehabilitated and reformed the lives of over 3000 people to date. And those people have in turn, affected the lives of countless others in a positive and constructive manner. And that could not have been possible if it wasn't for the love and true power of this extraordinary Woman that lay before you today. Her love is stronger than death, and therefore she can never die.

"SHE POSSESS TRUE POWER"She is a woman who possess true power. What is true power? True power is the ability to define reality, and have others accept, reality as she defines it, as if it was their very own. Cecelia McEachin is a master at defining reality. She decided to create a New Family Reunion. And that is written in her will.

She has said and demonstrated many things that I would come to understand later in life. Momma would always say to me:

"SON, NEVER MAKE EXCUSES MAKE ADJUSTMENTS"

She has a mother's wit that is incredible. And all of us know that she is one woman that you cannot run game on. Although from time to time, she would let you think you have her fooled. Then she would give you that serious stare of hers, and by her stare, you would know that you've just been had. And God knows that I received that stare from her many times.

"MOMMA KNOWS HOW TO LOVE"

I can remember one time when I was playing football in the street. One of the children I was playing with pushed me when I was trying to catch a pass. I fell into the curve head first and bust the side of my head open. The children I was playing with ran because they thought they were going to get in trouble. And I staggered into the house hollering for Momma, blood all over my face. Our telephone was off at the time so Momma couldn't call the ambulance, and her pride wouldn't let her ask any of her neighbors if she could use their phones. So Momma got her pocket book, and she walked her son to the hospital. I was tired and dizzy from the trauma to my head, so halfway to the hospital; Momma picked me up and carried me the rest of the way. After I was treated and released Momma was tired, so we slept in the hospital until morning, then we walked back home. This was in the middle of the summer and it was extremely hot. Momma and I would repeat this process on numerous occasions. One time, in the middle of winter I broke my right index finger. It was freezing cold this particular day. Me and my Momma, once again, are walking to and from the hospital. I guess Momma didn't have enough money for us to catch the bus or a cab to the hospital on those occasions. And we all know, unless you're literally dying, the Ambulance services has never been a friend to the hood. Other then chastising me for not being more careful when I was playing, Momma didn't complain. And she didn't ask for help. The lessons she taught me here are many:

1. There is no greater love than the love a mother has for her son, and no matter what she is going through she will sacrifice all that she has for her child;

2. Family takes care of Family, and no matter what family never forsakes family.

3. When all else fails, do for self. Never depend on others to do for you what you can do for yourself; and,

4. We often have to function in life based on the cards that society deals us, and you can't play a hand that you don't have.

Now I know what Cecelia McEachin meant when she use to say: "Never make excuses make adjustments".

I declare to all, that before I leave this physical plane of existence, the world is going to know who Cecelia McEachin is. Because I am Cecelia McEachin, and so are all of you.

To my Aunt Na Na, Ms. Frances McEachin-Collins, you are also my mother. And my sisters, my children, and their children will forever treat you as such. And I say to you today, that I am proud to be your son.

IF I COULD GET YESTERDAY BACK

If I could get yesterday back,

I would always think before I act,

Because there is always more to the story,

Only time reveals the facts

If I could get yesterday back,

I'll be more patient with the puzzles of life,

Because lack of patience distorts life's picture,

And hides the guiding light

If I could get yesterday back,

I would never let go of her hand,

Not even when her touch feels rough,

That's just love we don't understand

If I could get yesterday back,

I'll take the bitter with the sweet,

I'll never complain and I'll enjoy the rain,

Like a child playing with Pop Sickles sticks in the street

If I could get yesterday back,

I would never prejudge you mother,

I would never complain about material things,

Because your love is like no other

If I could get yesterday back,

You would know that I love you more,

And when you asked me not to leave your house,

I would have never walked out of loves door

If I could get yesterday back,

And I knew that would be our last conversation,

I would repeat the very same words to you mom,

I am proud to be your creation

There is no greater honor then to be your son,

There is nothing in this world that can compare,

Cecelia McEachin you and I will always be one,

And I know that wherever I am you will always be there

But Momma, I still wish I could get yesterday back.

CONTENTS

INSIDE the MIND

INSIDES

MIND

Word of the Week

WORD 1

"CREATE A NEW REALITY"

We as men must condition ourselves for a cause that is greater than any one person, a cause that is beneficial to the whole. Unfortunately, most men in prison can't see past their group affiliation and they can't see supporting people who are from outside their geographical location, which blinds them mentally and stagnate their progress as men. Men can associate with those they want to associate with, but men should not adopt tunnel vision and associate with one particular person or group (religious or otherwise) especially when that group or individual interferes with the ideas of peace, unity and making this compound (or the world) a better place for all men to exist. An ignorant man is an enemy to himself and others. Those who would foster disunity among men are an enemy to the cause of unity and peace. They are not fit for leadership. We are all struggling for balance and there are many obstacles placed in our own path through self imposed ignorance. Peace breeds Peace, Unity breeds Unity, and Respect breeds Respect. So demonstrate Peace, Unity and

Respect toward all men and you will receive it in return. It will take MENTAL CONDITIONING. If you change your mental condition you can create a new reality.

WORD OF THE WEEK: CREATE A NEW REALITY

May Peace and Blessings be upon you, Your Brother and Humble Servant.

M. Djhuiti Menes. "The Struggle Continues"

WORD 2

"HOW DO YOU WANT TO BE REMEMBERED?"

Men in prison must never allow themselves to get comfortable. If you allow yourself to get comfortable, the minute your comfort zone becomes threatened you will begin to sell pieces of your integrity to stay comfortable. With each piece of your integrity sold a part of your character collapses, all the way to the point where you can't be trusted, not even by the person you see in the mirror. You are then, in sellout mode. One of many reasons people sellout is because their perception of reality is flawed, and or has been tainted by beasts posing as human beings. These beasts train people to roll over and do tricks as if they were dogs. The dog trainer therefore forces the dog to accept a reality that is not the dogs. If you've ever seen a pit bull, or any dog for that matter, nurturing a kitten as if it was of its own litter, you've seen a dog that has been robbed of its reality. And so it is with people who compromise their morals and principles for the sake of being comfortable. When people place more value on material gain than on human life that peoples reality has been tainted. If you're a so called street dude, or a revolutionist and you place more value on staying out of prison then on staying true to the people who trust you, you're unworthy and can't be trusted. As far as men in prison, when you place more value on freedom or staying out of the hole than on principle, and more value on winning at the sake of losing a friend, you're a prostitute and can't be trusted as far as you can spit. Life and all its pleasures are not so important that a person should sellout just to have it. The one who would sellout does not know the reality of what exists beyond the grave. When you are dead and gone how will the sellout be remembered. They will be remembered as a whore to all who stood and still stand on principle. How do you want to be remembered?

WORD OF THE WEEK: HOW DO YOU WANT TO BE REMEMBERED?

May Peace and Blessings be upon you, Your Brother and Humble Servant;

M. Djhuiti Menes. "The Struggle Continues"

WORD 3

"LET'S STOP KILLING OURSELVES"

Every move that a man makes should be a calculated move toward a greater cause, or he shouldn't make the move at all. Men who move without purpose move without a cause, and men who move without a cause have no foresight because they only focus on the immediate. "The Immediate is Often an Enemy of the Ultimate". Most men are rebels, which in the sense that I am using the word means to be in a constant state of mental and oftentimes physical rebellion. It's OK to rebel but who and what are you rebelling against? What is your purpose? What kind of picture does each act in the scenes of your life produce? In other words, if your life were the pages of a book for the world to read what would be in your book? Overstand this; you are a publisher. Your every deed, your every act, and every word that comes out of your mouth is being published in the minds of the people you encounter. What kind of book are you writing? Whether you know it or not your book is constantly being read, let it not be said that you are an emotional wreck, rebelling against yourself, callously making moves "WITHOUT A JUST CAUSE" . Each move that a man makes that is not a calculated move toward a greater cause could be self destructive and an act of suicide; he just simply slowed down the process, as we do often do. I'm tired of dying, aren't you?

WORD OF THE WEEK: LET'S STOP KILLING OURSELVES

May Peace and Blessings be upon you, Your Brother and Humble Servant;

M. Djhuiti Menes. "The Struggle Continues"

WORD 4

"UNNECESSARY AGGRESSION"

Unnecessary aggression is a sign of weakness and mental instability. When a person is injured mentally; that person deals with the injury based on his or her level of understanding. If the injured person is ignorant their ability to deal with the injury is limited to how they have been taught, trained and conditioned to deal with the "perceived" injury. In other words, their ignorance and or mental limitations renders them mentally unstable or unable to respond to the (problem) injury rationally. The unstable mind then uses acts of aggression as an art to express itself. It is a mind that is underdeveloped and trapped in the animal stage of its existence. It refuses to listen to reason and functions solely on instinct because most animals cannot be reasoned with. Survival of the fittest is all they know. If you find yourself in the presence of individual (s) who uses unnecessary aggression as a form of expression, you are in fact in the presence of hyenas, i.e., animals who function without purpose or reason. These people (in this stage of their development) should be avoided. To stay among them is an act of insanity because you're asking to be abused and disrespected.

WORD OF THE WEEK: UNNECESSARY AGGRESSION.

It is a sign of weakness and mental instability.

May Peace and Blessings be upon you, Your Brother and Humble Servant;

M. Djhuiti Menes. "The Struggle Continues"

WORD 5

THE TWO PIECE

"ORGANIZED CONFUSION & IGNORANT HYPOCRISY"

Lack of organization and structure among any group of people leads to chaos and confusion. Mix that with headless or so called leaders who lack direction and what you have is a recipe for disaster. Especially when these Headless Horsemen have full grown men/children who are impulsive reactionaries with bipolar disorders under their leadership. These men/children throw temper tantrums for sport and play. Unfortunately, these men are at war with themselves. Men who are at war with themselves accomplish nothing but self destruction. This self destruction is an act of suicide caused by a deep seeded fear. Most men/children are afraid and or lack the mental capacity to effectively confront their real oppressor so they target and attack the oppressed, i.e., people suffering from the same *"Hell of Oppression"* that they're suffering from. When the oppress attack the oppress the oppress becomes an agent of his original oppressor; the oppressed is then practicing the age old art of *"Ignorant Hypocrisy"*: Unconscious of the force behind your actions but totally aware of your deeds; The victim of an unseen Hand/Force; carrying out objectives that is contrary to your existence, objectives that contributes to your demise and or the demise of one's own people: *Unconscious Ignorance.*

So now what? What must be done? Men in positions of leadership must create a charter. That charter must include, rules, regulations, principles and procedures, and a Code of Conduct; Moral Ethics. All of which should be carried out and enforced by convicts; we don't need the law to solve our problems. You dig!

May Peace and Blessings be upon you, Your Brother and Humble Servant;

M. Djhuiti Menes. "The Struggle Continues

WORD 6

"GEOGRAPHICAL INSANITY"

Geographical Insanity: Representing and being willing to die for a Geographical location or group (a ghost) without thought or reason, concern or consideration for life or the well being of human beings: "Geographical Insanity".

Where we are from or what we claim does not make us different from any other convict; in the sense that we have all been convicted of some criminal offense. No matter your skin color, your religion, or what your perception of reality may be, we are all the same. We are one race, one people, a new race of people called "CONVICT". From that perspective all of us have one religion and this is an eight digit fed number, unless you're undercover agent or an agent provocateur working on behalf of those people to cause confusion among convicts? Check yourself!

If you suffer from geographical insanity you can actually be an agent and unconscious of the fact that you're an agent. Do you be saying things like, *"I don't like him because he's from here or there; or I don't like him because he is with this or that group"*. If this is you, you're an agent, you just don't know it. Stop working with them peoples.

WORD OF THE WEEKS: THE 2 PIECE.

1.) we must alleviate organized confusion, destroy ignorant hypocrisy, and; 2.) kill geographical insanity.

May Peace and Blessings be upon you, Your Brother and Humble Servant;

M. Djhuiti Menes. "The Struggle Continues"

WORD 7

"OFF THE CHAIN"

Every moment is a struggle. As long as you are struggling you know that you're alive. So struggle is good. Hard trials are necessary to establish truth. We often feel pain and suffering because of our past experiences and we often regret some of the choices we've made or think we've made during the course of our lives.

We are not guilty. In reality "we" really haven't done anything wrong. So many strong Black, Red, Brown, Yellow and poor White men were and are the victims of oppression and psychological warfare; Exploited! How can we be sorry or feel guilty for anything that was done with the mind of the enemy on our shoulders? That is rhetorical question so there is no need to answer it. Basically, we've been raped mentally.

We were indoctrinated. That indoctrination was/is so atrocious and so wicked that it blinded us to the reality of who we truly are and what we stand for. Once we begin to see ourselves for who we truly are the enemy knows that we will begin to see them for who they truly are. When we begin to see them for who they truly are, we will be beyond their control. And when they can't control us, they intimidate, eliminate/exterminate, terrorize and or isolate us. In other words, they neutralize all potential threats. This neutralization takes on many forms.

We know the enemy deliberately place drugs in the Black community then have Black men competing with each other for a piece of the so called American Dream while at the same time trying to escape the nightmare that we're trapped in. The young Black man, having no real skills to do anything else, sell those drugs to "street treat Black male frustration". As sister Frances Cress Welsing put it, *"the Black man is made to take the blame"* for all of the atrocities that takes place as a direct result of covert, and often overt malicious acts committed by the controlling forces, i.e., the powers that be. It's all an elaborate scheme, of which poor Whites are also infected and affected by. It's a part of their play book. And when you don't play along they try to destroy you. Especially when they can't break you.

14

Then they fill the minds of the young Black females with the idea that they are nothing but a sex object, and that good sex is the only way to get and keep a good man. This translates in her mind as the only way to survive. As a result of these females trying to survive, they express love through sexual acts, never taking into consideration that with each sexual act, especially when those sexual acts are performed in vain and out of complete ignorance, a part of them die. And if the female gets pregnant, death followers, because an ignorant woman and a foolish man produces a stillborn that is physically alive, but will possibly be raised spiritually and morally deaf, dumb and blind. THE BLIND LEADING THE BLIND. "Let it marinate", as Brother Anthony Muhahammad of Mosque #4 always said. It is an ugly scene, one that we have seen too often.

We must gain a better understanding of who we are and how we think, To understand who we are we must know ourselves. We must study ourselves and examine the origin of our behavior, chronicling the events of our lives from the past to present. What we will discover is that with each stage of our development (consciousness) an evolution takes place in our minds which manifest in reality. What we are today is not what we were yesterday, and what we will become tomorrow is not what we are today. Tomorrow, we will be greater men than we are today because we are greater men today then we were yesterday. If you're not growing mentally you are in a stage of regression and full of regret.

We regret some of the choices we've made until we understand that the choices we made in utter ignorance, the choices we made in complete mental darkness, are not really choices at all, they are instinctive reactions. Man, in the animal stage of his existence does not really have free will. He is willed, and that which wills him makes choices for him even though he may think he makes them for himself. Only when man reaches his spiritual or the divine stage of his existence (God Consciousness) can he begin to make decisions (Choices). Therefore, many of us have never made a choice in our lives, only instinctive reactions; that is what animals do. Most unconscious people are in the animal stage of their existence. Animals can be trained. That is why we must break away from the chain/leash. Only then will we literally be, "OFF THE CHAIN".

WORD OF THE WEEKS: BREAK THE LEASH AND GET "OFF THE CHAIN"

May Peace and Blessings be upon you, Your Brother and Humble Servant;

M. Djhuiti Menes. "The Struggle Continues"

WORD 8

"I DON'T LIKE THE WAY YOU LOOKIN AT ME"

When has the way a person looks at you ever hurt you?
If looks could kill, half the population of the earth would
be dead. We should never judge a person by their facial
expressions or their appearance. I've seen snakes and wolves
smile and hug a person and tell that person they love them,
then stabbed the person they said they loved in the back and
speak ill of that person with the same breath. They appeared
harmless, but turned out to be more dangerous than those
who walk around with frowns, grits and mugs all day. People
who frown, grit and mug all day are only asking for help.
They have a lot bottled up inside of them and need someone
to talk to, but they don't say anything because they feel that no
one can be trusted. So their pain is internalized and manifests
itself outwardly in the form of frowns, grits and constant
mugs.

Nobody likes a Mug shot because most of them appear ugly.
But it's only a mask to cover up some deep pain or suppressed

emotion (s). If you receive *"MUG SHOTS"*, understand that it is just a mask so don't trip. Try speaking and offering a kind word to the *Mugger*. You just might save a life. At the same time, if you are a *Mugger,* you should know that it takes less facial muscles to smile than it does to Mug/Frown. Try another form of expression because I'm tired of getting robbed; let's talk about it. The one thing you should never say to a MUGGER is; *"I DON'T LIKE THE WAY YOU LOOKIN AT ME"*. If you say that, you both have just been robbed, and it's a whole lot of broke dudes on this compound. (LOL)

May Peace and Blessings be upon you, Your Brother and Humble Servant;

Brother M. Djhuiti Menes. "The Struggle Continues"

WORD 9

"IDENTITY THEFT"

Identity Theft, aka Swagger Jackers, aka Perpetrating the Fraud. Some people want to appear to be something or someone they are not. They will even go so far as to tell you stories about what other people did or are doing, making it seem as if they themselves have done or are doing it. Perpetrating the Fraud: Some people will go so far as to make up stories or fantasize about things that they have done when in reality those things have never happened. What's crazy is that these people have convinced themselves that the stories they tell are true. And some will even put their lives on "THEIR TRUTH", which is in reality a LIE. Why would a person make up stories about themselves that are not true? Many reasons; low self esteem, lack of knowledge of self and or they trying to accomplish something that the people they are lying to don't know about. No matter the case, it is a form of deception.

Swagger Jackers: Those who seek to deceive, in most cases, cannot be trusted; especially when they have deceived themselves. How can you trust a person who can't trust themselves? You can't. In prison you can be all that you want to be, unless someone knows you from the street, your claims can go unchallenged. You had this and you had that, you did this and you did that. Why talk about it if you had it. Thinking people are not impressed with what you had and what you did. They are impressed by what you're doing now that leaves an impression on them. At the same time thinkers don't tell it.

May Peace and Blessings be upon you, Your Brother and Humble Servant;

M. Djhuiti Menes. "The Struggle Continues"

WORD 10

"YOU CAN'T HOLD HER YOU CAN MOLD HER SO STOP WORRYING ABOUT THE BOX"

You can't hold a woman. You can mold a woman. To mold her you must first create a bond with her based on integrity and team work. The relationship must be principled, and it is on those principles that a foundation should be built. *Stop worrying about the box (Her Sex Object) you lost the key to that with incarceration,* so stop trying to lock her up with you. Just build a strong foundation and a good bond and strong communication with her. With a strong foundation and a good bond/communication the sky is **not** the limit; when man and woman work together in harmony they produce space shuttles that travel beyond this world. This space shuttle is not produced by man and woman through gratification of the senses, for those are things that pass away. It is/was produced when man and woman work together in **Common Sense**. Common Sense is a pattern of thought that is usually produced through experience and reason. *When a man does not function with experience and reason (Common Sense) a woman sees* *that man as an object floating in space being wasted by time, and therefore, a waste of her time.*

A man should study himself and his woman. Once he master himself there is nothing beyond his scope of influence. The wise man know that most women represent a jewel that has exploded into many pieces. Each piece must be nurtured and put back into its proper place. These pieces cannot be discovered, so the wise man does not search or pry; he allows time to reveal the pieces to him. As each piece reveals itself, the **Wise** man has the proper knowledge, overstanding and wisdom to put the broken pieces back together and the missing pieces to the puzzle back in place. **Then the whole picture becomes clear to him.** Signs and symbols are for those with eyes to see and ears to hear. Can you see? Can you hear? Well why are you trying to maintain control of the box from prison? Wise men know better than to concern themselves with things that are beyond their sphere of control. When I begin to lose focus that is what I do: "I draw a circle." Inside of the circle, I write down the things that I have complete control over. Outside of the circle, I write down the things I don't have complete control over. Then I focus on the inside of the circle. I don't block out the things on the outside. I just realize I don't have complete control over things outside of the circle, including **"The Box."** Where she been, why did she do this and didn't do that, and accusing and disrespecting her ain't gone get it. That will only push her away. If you read and study the right information and exercise some self discipline you can offer her words of wisdom and advice so powerful that all she will think about is your mind. Knowledge is to the mind what food is to the body; **Nourishment! So nourish her mind. You can't hold her you can mold her so stop worrying about the box. Cause you ain't got the key no more; Champ!**

May Peace and Blessings be upon you, Your Brother and Humble Servant;

M. Djhuiti Menes. "The Struggle Continues"

WORD 11

"DECEPTION"

Deception: Wicked is the mind that practice it. **Sharp** is the Mind that sees it. **Keen** is the mind that comprehends it. Intelligent is the mind that has the mental capabilities to overcome it. And conscious is the mind that does not practice it: **DECEPTION.**

Deceivers often create storms. It takes strength and will power to remain steady and calm through those storms. Long gone are the days when honesty and honor is the order of the day because this world has corrupted all but a few. Those who managed not to become corrupted by this world are seen as outcast or abnormal in the eyes of the corrupt. Deception corrupts the unsuspecting mind especially when the deceiver is trusted.

The deceived does not see things as they are because he or she may be blinded by loyalty, and therefore, refuse to examine the behavior of the deceiver. It is hard to deceive a wise man.

Although in some instances a wise man can be deceived. The wise man sees things as they are and not for what they appear to be, just as the fool can see nothing but the pebbles of their own mind. Deceivers are fools, and will even wave their pebbles before the wise man as if they are something to behold. The wise man just sighs, and feels pity for the one who tries to deceive him. The wise man knows that the deceiver is dead and does not know he's dead. Deceivers think they got all the sense, and to some extent that is true because they function within the five senses and without reason. Deceiving others is self defeating.

May Peace and Blessings be upon you, Your Brother and Humble Servant;

M. Djhuiti Menes. "The Struggle Continues"

WORD 12

"REAL GANGSTER"

REAL GANGSTERS: indoctrinate people into a wicked mind set that is subversive to their interest and serves the purpose of the **REAL GANGSTER"**. There are no *Real Gangsters* in prison. *Real Gangsters* have never been inside of a prison. Some of us put in a little work **(HURT SOMEBODY)** in prison or on the street then call ourselves *Real Gangsters*. **SHUT YOUR MOUTH!** You are delusional and need a reality check. *Real Gangsters* design prisons, and are the chief architects and orchestrators or our mass migration inside of these mass industrial prison complexes, aka, modern day slave plantations. *Real Gangsters* have three primary concerns, money, power and control. They focus on the object. They are not concerned with what race you are, but they will play the races against each other to maintain their money, power and control. *Real Gangsters* create and pass laws that they enforce but don't honor. *Real Gangsters* are the masters of a concept called **"PROBLEM, REACTION, and SOLUTION"**. They create the **"PROBLEM"**, to get a desired **"REACTION"**, so they can implement a **"SOLUTION"** that the people would have never accepted if the *Real Gangster* didn't create the problem. *Real Gangsters* order and carry out the assassinations of people on foreign soil in Sovereign Nations. It ain't no *Real Gangsters* in prison. You ain't no **REAL GANGSTER, SO SHUT YOUR MOUTH!**

May Peace and Blessings be upon you, Your Brother and Humble Loyal Servant;

M. Djhuiti Menes. "The Struggle Continues"

WORD 13

"REAL GANGSTER PART 2: THE BREAK DOWN"

Some of you seem to think that you are *Real Gangsters*. You may be a G.A.N.G.S.T.E.R., which stands for, *Genocidal Advocate, Naive Goon Struggling To Erase Righteousness*. But there are no *Real Gangsters* in prison. To even want to be considered a *Gangster* is a sick mentality. Some of us manage to make the transition from Boys to Men. Some of us grow old but we don't grow up, clinging to boyhood until the day we die, allowing the ego to guide us through our short journey on earth. We have become so concerned with what our so called friends think that we neglect the wisdom of our Mothers and those who truly love us. When it's all said and done, Mom is usually the one that is in your corner; **AND SHE AIN'T FUC** WIT NO GANGSTER**. *Ya Dig!* You don't play the Gangster role when dealing with her and the people who truly love you, like your children, your grandmother, your dear uncles and aunts. If you are not willing to accept the challenge to change then why are you always telling *Momma* that you changed. Stop Faking! When you call home tell Momma how

Gangster you really are. She ain't trying to hear that SH**. And neither are your love ones. So shut your mouth! **IT AIN'T NO REAL GANGSTERS IN PRISON**. However, there are a few brilliant men in here, most of which don't even know they're brilliant. But it ain't no gangsters in prison.

May Peace and Blessings be upon you, Your Brother and Humble Loyal Servant;

M. Djhuiti Menes. "The Struggle Continues"

WORD 14

"KEEP YOUR WORD"

If you give your word to someone you should keep it. If you are not sure you can keep your word then you should not give it. The term *WORD IS BOND* comes from men who saw giving their word to a person as offering that person a part of themselves. When you break your word you break *THE BOND*, and from that point on your words carries no weight and have no impact. A picture may be worth more than a thousand words but when you keep your word the picture you paint of yourself says one word to everyone who you see you: TRUE. When you break your word the picture of you is shattered into a thousand pieces, and like a broken mirror it gives off a thousand different reflections, then you're seen as a chameleon bending to circumstances and compromising for gain. You're applauded for your performance but everybody laughs at you in secret because you broke *THE BOND* when you didn't keep your word. You might have borrowed and owe a person $2000 or 2 stamps and never paid him back. He may or may not get your head crack for the $2000, and he may not sweat the 2 stamps, but in his mind he is saying; that is a petty dude, while smiling at you on the outside.

There is a saying, *"Universal Law Govern all Events"*. The universe functions in order, and it is in that order that *Universal Law Govern all Events*. Every time you break your word you are *OUT OF ORDER,* and the events that follow a broken word are never good even though things may seem "All Good". What seems to be seldom is, but your word defines you when you break it and when you keep it.

May Peace and Blessings be upon you, Your Brother and Humble Loyal Servant;

M. Djhuiti Menes. "The Struggle Continues"

WORD 15

"HATERS AND SALT SHAKERS"

When a man lacks self confidence and is not sure of himself he often display it by making negative or untrue statements about other people. He usually never looks for the good in anyone because he can see no good in himself and he therefore leaps at the opportunity to hate without cause. He is shallow and has no real sense or self worth.

{Dr. Joy Degruy Leary, Ph.D. said, "we arrive at our self-concept or self-esteem" through the following thinking pattern; "I am not who I think I am, and I am not who you think I am. I am who I think that you think I am".}

Some people deserve criticism because it gives them a chance to take a good look at themselves. But a HATER will ridicule a man he don't even know. When someone knows a person and is supposed to be cool with that person, then speaks ill of that person, he is usually speaking with his emotions and is probably in some kind of pain. Emotions in that case is a weakness in the affairs of men, because it often distorts reality and blurs a man's vision, at which point, he becomes a "**Hater and Salt Shaker**". When he passes the **Salt** around the table, the weak among him will consume so much that they catch high blood pressure then outwardly display illnesses that come with the dis-eased mind. Conscious people can see it. Smart people push away from the table so they won't become infected.

People who have self confidence are not **Haters**. Intelligent people don't eat that kind of **Salt,** and the wise avoid **"Haters and Salt Shakers"**.

May Peace and Blessings be upon you, Your Brother and Humble Loyal Servant;

M. Djhuiti Menes. "The Struggle Continues"

WORD 16

"PERFECTION"

The goal of man is to reach perfection, but some believe that perfection cannot be achieved. I see perfect people all around me. These people just don't know that they're perfect because they have been taught that perfection is doing everything right and never making any mistakes. Perfection, in reality, is acknowledging your mistakes and not making the same mistakes twice.

Perfection is not being afraid to apologize when you're wrong. Perfection is not always being correct but always trying to do the right thing based on what you know and the principles you follow. Perfection is standing on those principles but listening to reason. Perfection is striving to be **Perfect,** and as long as you're striving to be perfect you've reached perfection. You may think you're far from perfect because you're in prison, and I'm sure you are constantly reminded of how imperfect you are. These reminders take on many forms; family, friends, associates, the courts; everybody weighs in on how far from perfect you are. Family is usually concerned, friends are sometimes weary, associates are often insecure, and the courts usually have wicked and hidden agendas. And others often judge you without knowing who you truly are, and once they get to know you they sometimes see you in a different light.

Perfection is simply trying to do the correct thing. Nothing more nothing less. I see perfect people all around me. Don't stop, keep trying.

May Peace and Blessings be upon you, Your Brother and Humble Loyal Servant;

M. Djhuiti Menes. "The Struggle Continues"

WORD 17

"PROPER PRISON ETHICS"

Friendships shattered, bonds broken, mended ties destroyed forever. All because one hot head can't control his temper and disrespects people. And to make matters worse, the men who are suppose to put the disrespectful child in check supports the temper tantrum.

Some of the same people who break bread and laugh together every day are now ready to kill each other over a "Child's Play". When they should be teaching the child/males among them **Proper Prison Ethics.** 1. Men respect all and demand respect; 2. Men choose their fights wisely, fools let fights choose them; 3. Never jeopardize the lives of others to feed your ego or for self gratification; 4. Never lie to a convict, be straight up, say what you mean and mean what you say; 5. Get as much education as you can and formulate a plan because men who fail to plan, plan to fail; 6. If you are wrong and an apology is in order, apologize. A sincere apology is a sign of growth and true manhood. 7. Never make a scene, because

INSIDE THE INSIDES MIND

it will draw tips. If your issue is with one person, speak with that person, don't play to the crowd. Playing to the crowd is a sign of weakness; 8. Always listen to reason, think before you act. Being an obsessive compulsive reactionary is a sign of a man that has a death wish with no regard for the whole; 9. "The strong rule the weak but the wise rule the strong. Braun is good, but Brain Power is Supreme."

May Peace and Blessings be upon you, Your Brother and Humble Loyal Servant;

M. Djhuiti Menes. "The Struggle Continues"

WORD 18

"KNOW THYSELF"

In order for man to understand himself he must have a solid understanding of history. A solid understanding of history gives him the eyes to see the full spectrum, as oppose to one color in the Rainbow of life. When a man learns his history and the history of other peoples {Not Fabricated History} he approaches life from a historical perspective without the prejudices that a lack of knowledge of self and others can infect the mind with. He is then freed from the prison of ignorance. Life, placed in a historical context becomes clear; the one thing that every life form on earth has in common is survival. History tells us that every life form wants to survive, and while the means and methods to bring about that end has been different throughout the ages, the goal of man has always been one; to survive. That is an undisputed fact. What then must take place if man is to continue to exist?

If beings from another planet attack (Earth) this prison and try to exterminate us all, we would set aside whatever differences we have because of our necessity to survive. We would immediately unite and plan a strategy to survive.

It often takes a tragedy for people to come together for a common cause. That is why so many people show up at funerals. We often celebrate the death of a human being that in life we took for granted. Let's start celebrating life as oppose to uniting because of some tragedy or ill circumstance. History has a role to play in the bigger scheme of things, know thyself and the purpose of all life, then maybe we will begin to live and let live.

May Peace and Blessings be upon you, Your Brother and Humble Loyal Servant;

M. Djhuiti Menes. "The Struggle Continues"

WORD 19

"PROPER PRISON ETHICS, THE BREAKDOWN"
(C.O.N.V.I.C.T. VS I.N.M.A.T.E.)

C.O.N.V.I.C.T. is an acronym for (C)onscious (O)f (N)onsense (V)ictorious (I)n (C)haotic (T)RIALS.

The **CONVICT** sets a pace and bits slow, i.e., does time with patience and learns his environment. He wants to see his surroundings as they are and not for what they appear to be. The **CONVICT** sees the entire picture and knows that the picture is constantly changing, so he adjusts his lens to see each circumstance as it is. The **CONVICT** knows it is important to be the message that he brings and to never wavier in the face of adversity. The **CONVICT** knows that there is no such thing as absolute knowledge and he is therefore constantly seeking knowledge, evolving. The words he speak is not to influence or persuade but to explain the world as he sees it without a prejudice or an ethnocentric view.

I.N.M.A.T.E. is the acronym for (I)gnorant (N)aive (M)ale (A)
gitator (T)elegraphing (E)verything.

The **INMATE** dives in head first without checking to see if
there is water in the pool. The **INMATE** cracks his head over
and over again because he refuses to listen. He thinks he
knows it all. The **INMATE** vision is blurred by wantonness
and his ears are plugged with stained words. He cannot see
reality nor can he hear its truths. He will only unite in the
name of self destruction but to live in construction he is afraid.
He will stand for nothing and die for anything. He is learned
ignorance.

Those who control the diameter of your knowledge prescribes
the circumference of your actions. Who taught you?

May Peace and Blessings be upon you, Your Brother and Humble Loyal Servant;

M. Djhuiti Menes. "The Struggle Continues"

WORD 20

"DON'T TAKE THE BAIT"

When a person has a problem with you for no reason that you can think of, you shouldn't address it or rack your brain trying to figure out why they have a problem with you. Once you address a person's unreasonable problem with you that person's problem(s) becomes your problem.

There is a practice called **FOOLS BAIT.** Fools Bait is similar to how a spider web works; once the unsuspecting prey has entered into the spider web, it is trapped, and then the spider immediately clamps down on it.

Example: A predator sits a newspaper on the table, then walks off and watch from a distance as potential prey tampers with the paper. The predator has a spotter { i.e., a person who will co-sign that the prey tampered with the paper.} The predator then approaches the prey and claims that something of value was inside the pages of the newspaper that was not really there. The predator then tells the prey "what was in the paper has to be replaced or else". The predator and the prey start arguing because the prey took the bait. The prey's foot is now trapped in the vice. It is the same thing when it comes to people with terrible attitudes and those who thrive off of conflict. If you feed into their madness you'll be trapped inside of their web; you'll become their prey. Feeding into their madness will do you more harm than good. You cannot advise misery, therefore you should never allow yourself to become a resting place for someone's misery. Ignore them if you can. But most importantly; **DON'T TAKE THE BAIT!**

May Peace and Blessings be upon you, Your Brother and Humble Loyal Servant;

M. Djhuiti Menes. "The Struggle Continues"

WORD 21

"THE F.A.M.I.L.Y."

(F)ORGIVING (A)CCEPTING (M)ENTALLY (I)NSYNC

& (L)OYAL (Y)EAR-ROUND

THE FAMILY is the most forgiving, exceptionally accepting, mentally in-sync & loyal year-round, not just when it's convenient.

Some of us focus on what's going on inside of prison and neglect what's real outside of prison: **THE FAMILY.** We get caught up in trials, tribulations and the politics of prison life; which cause us to disrespect, disregard and neglect the people who care most about us: **THE FAMILY.** We gossip, spread rumors, slander, and make false accusations about each other just to be accepted by our peers, most of which are disloyal.

Some of us back stab one to please another, when in reality we're putting the knife in our own back. How? By putting so much focus into prison life, you become drained and have no energy to put into **THE FAMILY**; you sell yourself short.

When you finally do write, email or call home they shun you because they feel that negativity and lack of positive energy resonating through you and it depresses them.

Then you look at **THE FAMILY** as if they ain't right, when it is you who have neglected **THE FAMILY** by not putting **THE FAMILY** first. Self examination is the key. Once we examine self we begin to see things clear, including the weeds in the gardens of our minds and in the minds of others. Get rid of the weeds and the garden will produce good fruit. Focus on the **"THE FAMILY"**.

May Peace and Blessings be upon you, Your Brother and Humble Loyal Servant;

M. Djhuiti Menes. "The Struggle Continues"

WORD 22

"THE REACTIVE MIND"

The reactive mind, What is it? How does it function? And how does it affect us. The reactive mind is within the subconscious mind but it has no consciousness. It is pure aggression embedded deep within the psyche/mind that functions without reason. In other words, it is an animal that functions instinctively. It has no friends, shows no partiality and it does not discriminate. It is reactive; readily responsive to a stimulus.

If you are reactive, when you're faced with a problem, the first thought that comes to your mind is destruction. That is because the reactive mind fails to contemplate and evaluate the problem. *DOGS ARE REACTIVE.* Some of us think that dogs are mans best friend. Some would even argue that dogs are more trustworthy than human beings, and in some cases they might be right. But if you feed any animal it will be your friend, especially when it's living in an environment that is foreign to its nature. Place the animal in its natural environment, deny it food, and you will become dinner.

When we function with the reactive mind we become like dogs, sometimes worse, because we allow instinct to override reason. Without reason it becomes a dog eat dog world, *Survival of the Fittest.*

Where there is no reason there is no conscience, where there is no conscience there is no sanity. And where there is no sanity there is only one thing left to say: *WHAT'S UP DOG!* I say it all the time.

May Peace and Blessings be upon you, Your Brother and Humble Loyal Servant;

M. Djhuiti Menes. "The Struggle Continues"

WORD 23

"CASEY ANTHONY > NOT GUILTY"

Why did so many convicts take special interest in her trial?

Why did so many convicts find her guilty before the verdict?

Why were some of you upset when she got acquitted?

You were interested because the mainstream media told you that you were supposed to be interested. Some of you found her guilty before the verdict because the media coverage tainted your thought process and made you believe that she was guilty, even though most of you seen the shoddy evidence presented at her trial.

Most of you watched her trial and found her guilty just like the public before the jury's verdict was announced. Found her guilty based solely on your emotions. Good thing those jurors didn't think like you and the general public.

Some of you were upset she got acquitted, you felt like someone should pay for what happen to the *toddler*. I sympathize for that baby and my heart goes out to the family, but I can't see how any convict would want to see someone get found guilty. Especially someone who was facing the Death Penalty. And I have heard many of you say that you wouldn't wish prison on your worst enemy. **Hypocrites!**

Someone said to me that she lied to the police. As if they have never lied to the police. They also said to me that she needs to explain the thirty days that past before the authorities were notified. I thought that defendants are innocent until proven guilty! I thought that the burden of proof was the government! It is bold face hypocrisy for a convict, (not government agents) who wanted the benefit of the doubt when they went to trial, to presume her guilty even after she got acquitted. *CASEY ANTHONY, NOT GUILTY!*

May Peace and Blessings be upon you, Your Brother and Humble Loyal Servant;

M. Djhuiti Menes. "The Struggle Continues"

WORD 24

"MAN UP!" SPECIAL EDITION

The opinions and views expressed in the **WORD OF THE WEEK** are solely Brother Menes. My views with respect to Casey Anthony are mine alone.

It is good that she got a fair shake, so stop hatin! What do you represent? Are you real or are you a great pretender perpetrating a fraud? What are the principles that you stand on? Do you follow those Principles?

You represent by what you do everyday. The only one who knows if you're real or fake is the man you see in the mirror. Some of us want so bad to change our circumstances that we would stoop so low as to want someone to end up in the same situation that we're in, which is not proper.

They say that there are two kinds of people in prison, those who told and those who wish they told. *I DON'T FALL IN EITHER CATEGORY.* I kept my mouth shut, manned up, went to trial and fought for my freedom and I am still fighting, so I have not lost. I WON. The time has not broke me, and will not break me. Don't break, don't bend, don't sellout. **PRINCIPLE OVER COMFORT!**

We win when we fight for our freedom. We win when we do our time and don't turn others in. We win when people go to trial and get acquitted. We win when we remain among the strong and unbroken. We win when we do our time and fight instead of crying. We win when we carry our own weight. We win when we stand up for the freedom and equity. We win when we learn who the real oppressor is and start fighting the machine and stop fighting and killing each other. We win when we man up.

SO MAN UP!

May Peace and Blessings be upon you, Your Brother and Humble Loyal Servant;

M. Djhuiti Menes. "The Struggle Continues"

WORD 25

"THEY SAY ANYTHING GOES" [SPECIAL EDITION]

I disagree! If you don't stand for something you will fall for anything. Hard trials are necessary to establish truth. There are men among you who have gone through the furnace of affliction, have been tried and tested, and has proven themselves to be worthy of the honor and respect that *REAL MEN* deserve.

At the same time there are also males among you/us who have been tested and failed miserably. Yet these males are accepted into many groups, (religious and non-religious) and are sometimes given a position of leadership, authority to govern the lives of *REAL MEN.* When that happens, *REAL MEN* see it for what it is; *"THE UNDER PLAY FOR THE OVER PLAY",* so they fall back from the group and keep their distance.

When I use the term *REAL MEN,* I am not speaking of males who will commit acts of violence, because most Rats can and will do that. I am speaking of men who can think, stand on street principles and hold true to those principles regardless of the circumstances. A man who respects Street Principles; "OMERTA: honors the Code of Silence…..and have a deep respect for Soldiers; a man who is not a Hater or a Salt Shaker; a man who respects thorough leadership and can lead when necessary; a man who never seeks to cause confusion; never petty; a man who is humble, yet has the Heart of a Lion: *REAL MEN.*

Who you keep in your inner circle says a lot about who you are. Failures allow jealousy and carnal desires to override common sense and reason, and therefore, failures often become ANYTHING. "THEY SAY ANYTHING GOES". I Disagree! What do you think?

[Note: the following is an excerpt (emphasis added) from a book that I wrote entitled *"Penitentiary Mind Games"*. The book is broken down into five parts and each part deals with the politics that takes place in prison. It addresses many aspects of prison life, from the head of the Bureau of Prisons and BOP decision making, to the Convict population and how the politics above affects the lives below and the affects that mass incarceration has on society.]

WORD 26

"PENITENTIARY MIND GAMES" (CELL ROTATION)

To those of you who have not done time in prison or are unfamiliar with what some prisoners have to go through to find a place to lay their head, i.e., a cell to occupy once they enter a Federal Penitentiary, peep the game:

When a prisoner enters a United States Federal Penitentiary, particularly on the West Coast, he has to find a prisoner who is willing to accept him in the cell. Acceptance is usually depended upon three factors; (1) Race, (2) Geographics and (3) Group/Gang Affiliation. For the most part people of different *Races,* from different Geographical locations, and from different Groups/Gangs usually do not occupy cells together. And the cells are so small no one really wants a celly. No man wants to live in a 7ft by 12ft cell with another man.

First of all, no one wants to, or should even have to live in a match box to begin with, let alone be forced to live in a match box with another man. The toilet stool, face bowl, bunks, table, chair and lockers are all inside of a sardine can called a cell. And when two prisoners have a little property the cell is even more cluttered. And it's even worse for men who are in the hole/lock down. During lock downs men are forced to occupy a cell together for approximately 165 hours a week, and sometimes 168 hours a week. It is only 168 hours in a week. The psychological effect's of such confinement is never even considered by congress, the court or executive prison officials. Why? Because most of them don't care.

Men are forced to endure (just like in the holes of slave ships) the smell when his celly defecate and pass gas. Prisoners/People are force to sometimes deal with a celly who refuses to take showers, has smelly feet and a terrible body odor to go with it. To make matters worse, if your celly has a bad case of halitosis, his bad breath will fog up the whole room like a fart. (LOL) It's funny but it ain't no joke. Especially when you have to deal with it for extended periods of time. Then there are those celly's that snore louder than a bull horn. Not to mention the possibility of being expose to TB, Influenza and other air born viruses by those with the whooping coughs. Those are just a few of the many reasons why some men don't want

to occupy a cell with another man and why all prison/penal

institutions should be single cell until prisons are phased out

completely. (It should be noted that prison staff often bring

germs into these penal institutions).

Prisoners/People are also forced to deal with the worldly

and other problems and vices a celly might have, such as

bad gambling habits, stealing, lying and cheating and other

kinds of trouble making. And if a celly is an ignorant bully

he will force his ways on his celly until the celly gets tired of

the nonsense, and end up doing harm to him, prison staff or

another prisoner. Lashing out is his way of escaping a harsh

reality made worse by bad policies and poor decision making.

WORD 27

"THE RAT FACTOR"

Then there is the RAT FACTOR. No one who is not a RAT wants to be in a cell with a RAT. This is another reason why most Convicts are reluctant to accept a person in a cell that he occupies. Once it is known that your celly is a RAT, people will look at you as if you knew, and/or accepted a RAT in the cell you occupy because you're one. The reality is that it can get you hurt, but for the most part you'll get shunned. How do you tell a man to accept a RAT when it was RATS that help put him in prison. I am not justifying criminal activity. What I am saying is this; when you get scratched, you don't tell the scratch to heal, the Supreme Intelligence of the human anatomy heals it naturally. And 90% of the prison population (allegorically speaking) is trying to avoid being scratched again. In other words, you don't close a cut by pushing a knife into it. Yeah I know, BOP policy says this and BOP policy says that. BOP employees break most of the BOP policies, especially when it comes to giving a convict justice. (They shipped me all over the country (Diesel Therapy) for teaching

Real Black History and fighting bad BOP policies).

Instead of separating RATS from real men, the Bureau of the Prisons spread them throughout the system. But most of the RATS are placed in minimum custody institutions or set free to trap more people. Most RATS are given immunity. The record should reflect that I used the term R.A.T.S as an acronym for (R)aping, (A)lluding (T)he (S)ystem.

May Peace and Blessings be upon you, Your Brother and Humble Loyal Servant;

M. Djhuiti Menes. "The Struggle Continues"

WORD 28

"MENTAL ILLNESS"

It is a tragedy when a prisoner(s) has serious mental and or psychological issues that require constant treatment by a trained professional and their mental illnesses is ignored and mocked. Prisoners with mental illnesses are often beat down by prison staff; mostly by stupid ass correctional officers who have numerous mental and psychological problems of their own, all of which they bring to work with them.

A consciously intelligent person/prisoner who have a celly that has mental and psychological problems will not allow prison staff to take advantage of his celly. He will, in fact, fight for, and in some cases die for a celly/person who is not mentally and psychologically sound when prison staff tries to take advantage of that person. All conscious convicts know that most prison staff take cold advantage of men and women with mental problems.

I, and many convicts, have had to fight for prisoners who have mental and psychological issues when prison staff took advantage of them. The point is, your celly's problem, and sometimes the problems of prisoners in the same housing unit as you can easily, and usually always do, become your problems. The BOP is most famous for collective punishment, and that can cause prisoners to harm each other.

WORD 29

"DEFENDING A MENTALLY ILL CONVICT"

In 2004 in Northern Neck Regional Jail, I was in the hole
(E-POD) with a Puerto Rican brother name Muopica. E-Pod
had 8 or 10 cells, half top tier, half bottom tier, all facing in one
direction, a tinted window bubble, right across from B-Pod,
and in between F and D-Pod. You can look out of the windows
of D and E-Pod and see the female Pod.

Muopica suffered from bi-polar disorder. Muopica needed
to be seen daily by a psychologist and he was supposed
to be given some kind of medication daily. This was all
documented facts that the prison staff, lead by a Major (Racist)
Hall, ignored. Here is how they treated Muopica's medical
condition: They brutally beat him down, stripped him buck
naked, took every piece of linen out of his cell, including
bedding, sheets, mattresses and all. They took his toilet paper
and turned the water off to the cell so there wouldn't be any
running water in the cell and the toilet wouldn't flush. He was
completely naked in a brick and steel cell.

They use to watch him from the camera they have in the cell, and taunt him through the two way speakers they have in the cell. They forced him to live in a cell with a toilet stool full of feces for days/weeks at a time. And they would often refuse to feed him. The smell was so terrible I can't even describe it. It was hard for me to breath just walking pass the cell. But I knew I had to talk to the brother and assist him as much as I could to keep him from losing it.

On the right corner, at the very bottom of the cell doors there is a small space/hole. I would slide food, flattened milk cartons and plastic bags with warm water in them in the corner and under his cell door when I came out for my hour rec. I would also slide sheets, towels and toilet paper under his cell door. Then I would sit outside of his cell, facing the Bubble (office) and talk to him for the remainder of my hour or rec. It wasn't long before the Northern Neck Prison Staff would pay two Punk Ass Rats to bring me a move. I won't go into details, but they never tried that again. I mop the floor with one of them and the other one ran before I could get to him. No convict should ever bring another convict a move for the police.

The E.R.T. EMERGENCY RESPONSE TEAM got there before I could get to the other one. I was set up. They wanted to isolate me away from all convicts, especially those who wasn't aware of their rights and those they were dogging, i.e. those prisoners whose constitutional rights were being violated. And it worked, they sent me to another Pod that only had three cells. I was in one of the cells, and some other guy (another mentally ill prisoner that the Northern Neck Staff abused) was down stairs in the other cell. The third cell was empty. This was another one of their hidden torture chambers. It was "O" or "P" Pod, "N" Pod was also a torture chamber. Northern Neck is a wicked joint, especially to convicts that ain't going for nothing. The point I am making here is that many Prisoners have stood up and fought for, and in many cases was killed at the hands of prison staff for standing up on behalf of themselves and their fellow convicts. And that says a great deal about people in prison, most of which society has written off and left for dead out of ignorance. Most of us have not lost our since of reason or purpose, and we have not lost, and will never lose our humanity.

WORD 30

KEEPING IT 100

I gotta keep it 100, there are some inmates in prison who are perverts and gun slingers, aka, jack'off artist. They don't want a celly because they want to be able to practice their perverted ways at will. That is, ejaculate/masturbate on the female officers/staff. Some perverts go around the compound (the penitentiary) looking for the best spots to masturbate on female staff. I call these individuals; **SNIPERS!** And they are of all Races, from all Groups, and from all Geographical locations. Most men in prison can't stand perverted ass snipers, and will beat their asses and run them up top, that is, send them to the hole if they catch them in act. Perverts don't want celly's and for the most part, no one wants to be in a cell with a pervert but a pervert. Unfortunately, some female staff often look at all Prisoners as if they are perverts because of what a few **I.N.M.A.T.E.S.** do. In reality **C.O.N.V.I.C.T.S.** are not perverts. There is a difference between Inmates and Convicts. Just for the purposes of clarity and making sure what I say is used in the proper context, here is what I mean when I use the term convict and the term inmate. "CONVICT" (C.O.N.V.I.C.T.) is the acronym for **(C)onscious (O)f (N)onsense (V)ictorious (I)n (C)haotic (T)rials. "INMATE" (I.N.M.A.T.E.) is an acronym for (I)gnorant (N)aive (M)ale (A)gitator (T)elegraphing (E)verything.**

Some of you may ask what makes a man so sick to the point where he would jack off/masturbate on female prison staff and think that his actions are normal behavior? **PRISON!** Why? Some men just can't handle the pressure of doing time in prison, and they break down and start functioning like savages. As my Brother Abdur R. Mahdi always say, *"it takes a beast to make a savage"*. While I don't agree with that behavior, I do recognize that it is a sickness created by circumstances. Some men lose all sense of reason and start acting like savages when they find themselves trapped inside of a cave.

Most behavior is learned behavior. Who taught you? Even if you learned from books, what you've read you learned from the mind of the individual(s) who wrote the book(s). Some men come to prison and learn from the prison environment.

WORD 31

"CRUEL AND INHUMANE"

A fool can see that its cruel and inhumane to subject a person to a 7ft by 12ft casket and expect him to think, act and function like a normal person. But that is not to say that there are not a lot of **ABERRANT MINDS** in society. I am sure you know many people in society that you think should be in prison or in some mental institution, just like I know there are many people in prison and mental institutions that should be in society. Everybody who seems to be sane is not sane and everybody who seems to be insane are not insane. However, some people who are placed in prisons are sane when they get here and are made insane by the circumstances of prison and the decisions made by prison officials. Just as some people who are placed in mental institutions are sane when they arrive and are made insane after being trapped and treated there for some time. Also, there are some sick and insane criminals in Authoritative positions (law enforcement) who exploit the people/masses and violate their rights, because having legal authority over people has made them sick and insane, if they were not already sick and insane. It's the wicked game that the machine plays to perpetuate it's existence.

WORD 32

"DEEPER THAN WICKED"

(To make matters worse, and prison far more dangerous
than it already is, the BOP has decided to implement a
policy in which they are going to start charging convicts for
each incident report, up to $500, or 75% of an inmates trust
fund, and a loss of privileges. Whoever thought of that is an
absolute asshole and damned fool! People will no doubt die
as a result of that dumb policy. *I WILL DO EVERYTHING
THAT I CAN WITHIN THE LEGAL RAMIFICATIONS OF
THE LAW TO FIGHT THE NEW BOP POLICIES, JUST AS I
HAVE FOUGHT THE BOP POLICES SINCE I HAVE BEEN IN
THE FEDERAL CUSTODY.* I am almost certain that the new
Draconian BOP Policies violates American Jurisprudence, as I
have become a very proficient litigator.)

I have not allowed the time to waste me nor have I wasted the
time. I read, read, read and read. I study everything, including
self.

The Executive Staff of the Bureau of Prisons are also studious. The Executive Staff of the Bureau of Prisons knows exactly what they are doing, and they know well the mental and psychological affects of incarceration. The Executive Staff knows and completely understand the affects of the their decisions because they have studied the plans and strategies laid down by the Chief Architects of these Mass Industrial Prison Slave Complexes called Penitentiaries, also known as Modern Day Slave Plantations. *THE SLAVE TRADE IS IN FULL AFFECT.* The Executive Staff, and most BOP staff for that matter, have agreed to participate in, and carry out, without mercy or remorse, thought or consideration for the welfare of the people housed in their care; the orders of the Plantation Owners. There are some Executive Staff who care about convicts and really do try to look out for the best interest of prisoners. But for the most part, the Executive Staff see prisoners as nothing more that a bunch of laboratory animals in a **MACROCOSMIC SCIENCE PROJECT.** Just as the Executive Branch, the Legislative Branch, and the Judicial Branch of the government view the American Public: As a major Experiment.

WORD 33

"SLEEP SHEEP"

Being in prison is just like growing up in the PROJECTS, that is, DA HOOD, because we're being constantly experimented on by those who run the laboratory. The question is, whose projects are they and who really benefits from the mass incarceration of the people? What is there to be gained, and what is there to be learned from these projects?

These large laboratory projects called Penitentiaries belong to the rich. The rich are given all of the contracts and provide all of the services in the Penitentiaries. The rich own 99.9% of the corporations that service all penal institutions in America and throughout the world. Prisons are a Billion Dollar Industry, and so are Prisoners. Therefore, Mass Incarceration is directly connected to the scheme called the American Dream.

Most of us who are incarcerated was led to prison through the pursuit of our dreams. Which in reality is a dream state and a deep sleep, also called the Spell of the Sheep. The mind set of the Spell of the Sheep gave and continues to give a wicked shepherd the opportunity to lead us astray. Some of us wake up after being incarcerated for a while, especially those of us who spend extended periods of time in the hole. And some of us continue to pursue the American Dream even after being trapped in America's living nightmare called prison. That is because some prisoners are still SLEEP SHEEP who refuse to wake up. Waking up means dealing with the reality of being trapped in a living hell, seeing Satan for who and what he really is, and fighting the devil on sight no matter where he rears his ugly head. Most of us just ain't ready for that. We'd rather pray and do nothing while we are being preyed on. Why? Because we're SLEEP SHEEP. We are, as Dr. York put it, *"UNDER THE SPELL OF THE SHEEP"*

WORD 34

"LABORATORY RATS"

Those prisoner/inmates who work with the administration against the best interest of C.O.N.V.I.C.T.S don't even realize that they are seen as nothing more that LABORATORY RATS by their Slave Masters. Once the Scientist/Slave Masters are finish experimenting with their RATS the Scientist/Executive Staff will expose the RATS, then drop them in the middle of angry CATS. The word C.A.T.S is used here as an acronym for (C)ourageous (A)ctivist (T)horough and (S)erious.

The Executive Staff use Mind Games to manipulate, and ultimately control Prisoners. They know that to control the mind of the Prisoner is to stop the REVOLUTION. One thing the Powers that be are well aware of is the fact that Prisoners are not afraid to function on the basis of the three R's, that is, prisoners are not afraid to **(R)ebel (R)efuse** and **(R)esist.** The powers that be also know that there is a distinct difference between the inmate and the convict. Some executive staff members will even go so far as to point out the difference between an inmate and the convict, and in Administrative

Orientation (A&O), they will let the prisoners know that they know what time it is. They know the Convict understands that written laws, rules and regulations are nothing more than another mans ideas on how a society should be governed. They know that the convict is honorable, and don't need the ideas of man to govern his conduct because the convict functions on a set of Principles that he will not break under any circumstance. On the contrary, they know that the inmate is unprincipled and function on the basis of the 3 S's, **(S) ubspected (S)nitches and (S)ellouts.** It must be noted that a snitch is an individual who breaks or has broken the law, cracks under the pressure of questioning, and then go so far as to let crooked law enforcement officers fabricate a statement/evidence and then testifies/test-a-lies to that evidence in the name of freeing themselves of accepting the responsibility for their actions. They commit crimes then snitch to get preferential treatment. Then they repeat the process over and over again. Hundreds of thousands and maybe even hundreds of millions has been placed in prison, lost their lives and separated from their family as a result of fabricated criminal cases by corrupt law enforcement officers and their counter parts; **SNITCHES!** Known in prisons as **LABORATORY RATS!**

May Peace and Blessings be upon you, Your Brother and Humble Loyal Servant;

M. Djhuiti Menes. "The Struggle Continues"

[Note: I first and foremost give special honors to all the stand up women convicts trapped off in the Penal Institutions in America and throughout the world. Next, I give honors to all the men in the Georgia State Prison and the men in the Pelican Bay Prison and other California State Prisons who stood up and continue to stand up for a cause. And all the Men and Women in the Shu's. (The Special Housing Units/Hole) in the Modern Day Plantations called Penal Institutions throughout America and the world. Just to name a few, I give a special honor to all the stand up men in the DC Jail, Upper Marlboro, Seven Locks, Dirty Ass USP/FCI Atlanta, USP Big Sandy, FCI Butner, USP and FCI Terre Haute, USP Victorville, where I am currently housed. And Special Honors to and all my Black, Brown, Yellow and White Brothers here who support the struggle and are stand up men. Special Honors to all the stand up men in USP and FCI Allenwood, USP Hazelton, USP Canaan, to all the stand up men in the SMU Programs in USP Lewisburg and those other wicked joints; To all the stand up men in USP Lompoc. USP Atwater, USP Lee County, USP Coleman 1&2, USP Florence, The Federal Super MAX > ADX, USP MC Crary, and Special Honors to all the stand up men and women in all the other Federal, State and Local Penal Institutions that I didn't name. From one convict too many: The Struggle Continues, Never Rat, Break, Bend, Fold or Compromise. We are only facing what others before us have faced, nothing more nothing less. Principles over comfort.]

WORD 35

"SPECIAL HONORS!"

SPECIAL HONORS to all the men who stood firm and are still standing firm. All the men who didn't break under pressure. Pressure bust pipes, but it also makes diamonds. Some men allow pressure to bust their wind pipes, often making a bad situation worse for themselves and for others. And some men stand firm under pressure, go through the struggle, and as a result of not breaking, turn into flawless diamonds. I know there are many men who held water and is holding true. I know that many of you took beefs to set others free. I know that many of you could be home if you would have told. But you didn't, you held fast, and that is worthy of honor and the utmost respect. SPECIAL HONORS! I got much love and respect for my comrades of all races and nationalities who are real men.

And Special Honors and respect to the men who are man enough to give me their honest opinions, sometimes good, and sometimes bad, on the WORD OF THE WEEK. I welcome your opinions and I care what you think because it helps me improve my service to God's people, that is, all of you. It is never my intention to disrespect any of you. However, I do know that some may become offended by what I write; you can feel free to let me know what's on your mind, I will listen with an open mind. And I will address your concerns in the WORD OF THE WEEK. Just don't ask me to respect dudes that ain't right. Other than that, it's all good.

Thanks to all of my honorable comrades in the struggle. You didn't compromise principle for comfort. You knew that compromising your principles would have been the beginning of the collapse of your character. And against all odds you stood firm and you're STILL STANDING. To all of my Comrades: SPECIAL HONORS!

May Peace and Blessings be upon you, Your Brother and Humble Loyal Servant;

Brother M. Djhuiti Menes. "THE STRUGGLE CONTINUES"

WORD 36

"STOP BEGGING"

Most leaders of today fail to put forth a strategy for change that doesn't involve begging. I can't stand hearing leaders beg because it implies depending on others to do for us what we can do for ourselves.

I am not oblivious to the fact that a large segment of America and the powers that be throughout the world are standing on, and sustaining their rule and power via inherited wealth. A wealth built on the backs of the indigenous peoples of the earth. I know that it is this same power and wealth that is used to continue to break the backs and the will of Black people and all oppressed peoples in general. YES THEY DO OWE US.

But at the same time, this power and wealth is also used to keep the masses blind, ignorant and at odds with each other; including White people. It is easy to blame ignorant poor Whites who have been mis-educated, misinformed and false indoctrinated as we often do, and not attack the power structure that keep their minds and the minds of the masses in a confused and a self destructive state. That is not to say that some blame is not justified, because some poor Whites can be so racist that it infects the mind of those who are the target of their racism. (Racism upsets the thought process of its victims. It breeds anger and a natural defense mechanism called hatred. Hatred produces absolute rejection. The race conversation is one that is long overdue.) And these poor Whites often protect powerful racist Whites, and by doing so poor Whites stand in the way of their own progress, often in the name of White power. Tricked by the Rich. The rich and powerful don't care about anything but maintaining their wealth and power, and rich Whites have proven that they will slaughter Whites to stay in power. That is why it is so easy for the United States Congress to declare war against other nations and send Blacks, Latinos and poor Whites into conflicts that have absolutely nothing to do with the troops who actually fight and die in these rich man wars. The point is, the rich and powerful, no matter what race they are, don't care about the poor.

The rich and powerful are without a doubt or contradiction an open enemy of the poor. Yet, the poor attack and terrorize each other. Very few among the poor attempt to attack the power structure of the rich and powerful. Not necessarily because they don't have the money and resources, because where there is a will there is a way. The poor don't attack the power structure of the rich and powerful mainly because most of them don't have the mental capacity, discipline and will power. Where there is no mental capacity, discipline and will power to fight, there is no desire to fight. At least not the real oppressor. But there are those poor fools who will attack and sometimes kill innocent poor people to treat their frustration that comes from the bag of tricks the enemy uses to fix their minds to self destruct. When any people are made and kept ignorant they are robbed of their ability to think and function rationally, and thus they are robbed of the ability to defend themselves. It's a dirty game and the powers that be play it well. That is why we beg instead of fighting.

To attack the power structure of the real oppressor, that is the rich and powerful, means that you/we, us, the poor, will have to suffer some hardships, and possibly be killed in the process.

A sacrifice that very few are willing to make because the rich and powerful are so dangerous and wicked that they will steal a baby's first tooth to maintain their power and control.

What does all of that have to do with leaders begging? As long as leaders beg and do nothing, those in power know that their comfort zone is not threatened. In fact, the powers that be will even fund an organization that feigns an attack against its rule. It called Political Theatre. But once a leader or an organization takes action to dethrone the rich and powerful, the rich and powerful will order their troops to attack that which threatens their rule. The rich and powerful will stop at nothing to maintain their control.

Most leaders, Black, White and of all other races talk a good game, but they really ain't about nothing but rhetoric. All show, melodrama. Say what you will about Fidel Castro and Maummar Gadhafi, but no one can dispute the fact that they are leaders of action. They spoke truth to power, stood on their word and fought. And I must add that Minister Farrakhan and the The Nation of Islam, in its Evolution, is a man and an organization that engages and attacks the power structure of the rich and powerful without compromise. Speaking truth to power in an intelligent and constructive manner. Fighting on behalf of all poor people in the United States of America and throughout the world.

In prison convicts who appear to threaten the rule of the prison power structure, whether it be the inmate power structure or the administrations power structure; are Segregated, Isolated and Regulated. But it's hard to Segregate, Isolate and Regulate a righteous convict on a mission for God. Especially one who can think. But even a righteous convict can be Segregated and Isolated, but never Regulated. The righteous never bow down, and for that reason they're feared by the powers that be. That are targets for assassination. So the powers that be just sit back and hope the feared fearless righteous one makes a mistake so they can capitalize on it. Just like "HATERS AND SALT SHAKERS", but worse.

The feared fearless righteous one never begs, he puts himself in a moral position to where he can make demands. He stands on his words and he does not break it. But there is one thing the feared fearless one never does; he never begs. I can't stand hearing leaders beg. Do for self. Stop Begging!

May Peace and Blessings be upon you, Your Brother and Humble Loyal Servant;

Brother M. Djhuiti Menes. "THE STRUGGLE CONTINUES"

WORD 37

RAW UNADULTERATED TRUTH (R.U.T.)

Some people can handle it, some people can't. It condemns some and saves others. But no matter what, it is what it is; RAW UNADULTERATED TRUTH. Lately quite a few people have been using the term, "I'M ON MAN TIME". It sounds slick, but what does it mean to be on man time? Frances Cress Welsing said that there are five categories of people: "MAN, WOMAN, BOY, GIRL AND BABY". If you're on MAN time that means you fall into the category of MAN. A MAN understands the importance of unity and order. A MAN does not think in individual terms because he understands the importance of the whole, recognizing that no MAN is an Island unto himself. In other words, when you were in the Baby stage of your existence, without the proper care you would have never made it to adulthood. And now that you're an adult, without the proper mentality, that is, man training, you'll never make it to man hood. You will grow old but will not grow up. A man is not afraid to commit to a cause. A MAN understands that being associated with a group, that has structure and wise righteous leadership is just as important as being a part of the President's Cabinet. A Man doesn't mock leadership, nor does he shun it when it's his time to lead. A MAN understands that he is a part of life's puzzle, he observes the whole, and becomes the piece that's needed to make the whole work, then steps into his place without complaining or interfering with progress. A man is what a man does. Men don't throw temper tantrums and make loud outburst when addressing an issue, because a MAN knows that in his every act a lesson is being learned by those who observe his behavior. Based on how you act, what lessons are there to be learned? What are you teaching, childhood or manhood?

Most of us claim manhood when in all actuality we are nothing more than grown children. I know for a long time I thought I was a man but was not. I thought being a man was being able to make babies and HAVE SEX WITH AS MANY WOMEN AS POSSIBLE. And the fruits of my labor was BABY MOMMAS DRAMA. Now I am finding out that I have children that I never knew I had. Fortunately, all of my children are brilliant, and they are God sent, very intelligent.

And there mothers are strong extraordinary women who I love dearly.

Now that I have had man training and I know most of what it is to actually be a man, I am constantly building strong ties with my children. And some of the decisions that I make in forging those ties do not sit well with my children or their mothers, but they are very necessary in order for them to have a bright future together.

The point I am making here is this, there are adult males in prison and in society who appear to be men physically but are immature mentally and have the mental capacity of children. These grown children need the guidance of men who have matured and have become men, not just through physical appearance but mentally and socially.

These children may not like the decisions that mature men make on their behalf but a man who cares is not going to knowingly make a decision that is detrimental to his children. A man is responsible because he has the mental capacity to

91

respond to almost any situation and circumstance that might present itself. If he is unable to respond he does not have a problem with seeking guidance from those who know. He knows that he does not know it all and that no one person has all the answers. Only fools think that they have all of the answers, and the fool should be avoided.

A man is not afraid to take charge, at the same time a man is not afraid to follow wisdom. And how does one follow wisdom? Plenty people have knowledge, and there is a great deal of intelligent people in this world. But there are very few who possess wisdom. In fact, there is less than one percent of the population of the Earth who actually posses wisdom, and I am being very generous in my calculations.

To follow wisdom is to first know what wisdom is: Wisdom is the application of knowledge and the exercise of righteous intelligence for the greater good of humanity. Wisdom is caring enough to make good sacrifices for people you don't even know and probably will never meet in your life time. Wisdom is making decisions and taking actions in the present that will benefit people in the present and the future. Wisdom is knowing that every living being is connected to every living being and if you hurt one being/thing you hurt all being/things, and if you help one being/thing you help all beings/things. You follow wisdom by observing its behavior and mimicking it. Here is wisdom, let him who understand it practice it. Manhood is wisdom.

May Peace and Blessings be upon you, Your Brother and Humble Loyal Servant;

Brother M. Djhuiti Menes. "THE STRUGGLE CONTINUES"

WORD 38

"REALITY CHECK"

REALITY CHECK is an acronym for (R)eal (E)vents (A)nd (L)ife (I)ntentionally (T)esting (Y)ou, (C)hecking (H)umane (E)motions, (C)onsciousness & (K)knowledge. The reality we see is usually not the reality that exist, but is often the reality we help create. When we embrace a reality that does not exist in fact, our frame of reference becomes flawed, and thus, whatever we say and do is said and done in ignorance. It's a constant struggle to stay balanced and function within reason, especially under these circumstances. However, we must realize that every situation that life places at our feet is only a test to see the mental and moral condition that we're in. How we respond to life's many tests says everything about who we are and what we stand for. If our principles are based on material wealth, items and nonsense outside of ourselves that has no real worth or value, then we are functioning in a false reality with a flawed view of what true wealth really is. True wealth is not in materials, it is having the mental capacity to deal with any situation effectively without doing harm to yourself, another person, and/or the society in which you live. True wealth is a good mental state of mind. When we become disconnected from reality we lose all sense of reason, placing value on things that are insignificant as it pertains to the Real Struggles that convicts face, such as fighting an unjust court system, fighting for better treatment, fighting for our freedom and fighting for stronger family ties. Instead, we're fighting each other. CHECK YOURSELF!

May Peace and Blessings be upon you, Your Brother and Humble Loyal Servant;

Brother M. Djhuiti Menes. "THE STRUGGLE CONTINUES"

WORD 39

"DEAR SPORT COAT"

Dear Sport Coat, why are you concerned with the fact that a woman is showing me love. Do you feel bad behind the fact that even from prison, she still feels me more than she feels you? You may be able to please her physically but you can never wear my shoes; I am me and you are you. I feed her soul, I make her feel whole and complete without touching her. You know when I hit the bricks what time it is. You hatin on me and playing with her emotions ain't gonna help you with her. Playing with her emotions only pushes her deeper into my arms. Let me give you some advice; cut your losses and find you another woman. Then treat that woman special, because the scars that you put on the woman who is now the target of my love you can never heal. All of your efforts to mend the wounds that you have placed deep within her heart will be fruitless. And all the sex in the world cannot replace the wisdom of a sincere man with an empathetic ear and a discerning heart. Sex is not everything to her. But there is a difference between want and a need. Sport Coat, you have a lot to learn. I soothe her mind, you disturb her peace. I cradle her heart; you crush her spirit. I listen to what she has to say; you ignore her. And when you Hate and Salt Shake on me to her, she looks at you with contempt, and says to herself, "how pitiful and weak it is for a so called man in Society to hate on a Real Man in prison". Then she asks you for some money so she can send me a money order. (LOL) But it ain't about the money, men in prison don't need money, it's about the Principle. Can you dig it Sport Coat? Well stop hatin, Charge it to the game!

"THE STRUGGLE CONTINUES" M. Djhuiti Menes

WORD 40

"NEVER GIVE UP!"

Some of us start feeling sorry for ourselves because we don't get letters or money from people in society. Then to make matters worse we often find ourselves surrounded by people who think negative, with views that coincide with a person that feels that they have nothing to lose. And we fit right in because we take on their mind set. At this point we have given in, and therefore, we have given up. How do we get out of this mental slump? I don't know, but I can tell you what worked for me. First, I decided that I was going to change my mind. In order to do that, I had to change my way of thinking. In order to change my way of thinking I had to put something worthwhile on my mind. I had to find something to live for, A Purpose! Then I had to either change the minds of the people around me or remove myself from the presence of Unconscious Minds. Then I drew the line. On the left side of the line I wrote down the things I hate about prison. On the right side of the line I wrote down the things that I could do something about, including the negative attitude that I adopted in prison. I then started doing something about the things on the right, and in doing so I started to feel good about myself. I started looking at things different and my reality started to change for the better. Then whenever I communicate with people, including people in society, they could feel the positive energy resonating from me. They begin to see me in a different light. In fact, they see me as the light. You are the light. Shine so that others may find their way. Never Give Up!

"THE STRUGGLE CONTINUES" M. Djhuiti Menes

WORD 41

"DEALING WITH THE LOSS OF A LOVED ONE"

We go through many trials in prison, and when things seem
to be getting a little better we often suffer another hardship.
There is almost nothing worse than losing a loved one,
especially a child or a parent. We can't attend their funerals
or pay our respects. How do we deal with the loss of a loved
one under these circumstances? There are no simple answers.
My aunt, my uncle, my grandmother and my stepmother
all passed within a period of 16 months. With each death I
was devastated. It's natural to grieve over the physical loss
of a loved one, but I became introverted. I didn't want to
be bothered with anyone. I shut down and held it all in. To
others, I appeared to be a bitter person. However, when I
began to express what I was going through, it helped me cope
with losing my loved ones. Then I realized that death comes
to us all and the only way to avoid death is to have never been
born. I also realized that those who are dear to me that have
passed are still a part of me spiritually and mentally. In me
they live and through me they will continue to exist. Just as

your loved ones who have passed will continue to live and exist through you. As long as you're alive they can never die. If you have suffered the loss of a love one, I pray that you find solace in these words. "As long as you're alive, you can help console others who may have suffered the loss of a love one. Your advice, a kind word and your condolences could be just what it takes to help a person cope, help them keep hope alive, stay focused and stay positive.

Respectfully, Brother M. Djhuiti Menes "THE STRUGGLE CONTINUES"

WORD 42

"LOGIC & REASON"

LOGIC & REASON is the practice of Common Sense. Where there is no LOGIC & REASON, common sense does not exist. And where there is no common sense, stupidity finds a safe house. Stupidity, is the friend of Misery, and Misery loves company. When Misery is the company of Stupidity they produce Ignorance. Ignorance is a friend to no one. Ignorance is the enemy of Consciousness. Ignorant people think they are smart, but they are unconscious, which makes them Fools. Fools are dangerous because they have no concept of Logic and they have no idea how to Reason. The Fool knows everything which means he can't be taught anything. A person that can't be taught anything is a Zombie; physically alive but mentally dead and don't know it. Mentally dead people cannot think, reason or comprehend. Mentally dead people hang out in grave yards, i.e., they surround themselves with the mentally dead. The mentally dead are ignorant. Ignorance has its own agenda. Ignorance is a blindfold or a veil that keeps a person from seeing. Those who cannot see, don't care. Those who don't care, function without a cause. Those who function without a cause, function without LOGIC & REASON. Logical: capable of reasoning or of using reason in an orderly well thought-out fashion. Reason: the power of comprehending, calculating, and thinking, especially in an orderly rational way. If you were to examine your own behavior, would LOGIC & REASON be what you practice daily? Is it LOGICAL to claim a cell that belongs to the government? Is it REASONABLE to claim a TV that is not yours that will be here when you're gone? Is it LOGICAL to run up a debt that you can't pay? LOGIC & REASON, do you practice it?

"THE STRUGGLE CONTINUES" M. Djhuiti Menes

WORD 43

"THE ART OF WAR"

In the book, "The Art of War", by Sun Tzu, it says "the Supreme Art of War is to Subdue your enemy without confrontation." The greatest enemy that man has ever faced is the enemy within. If man can manage to subdue that enemy, he'll find/gain internal peace. It is the internal that moves the external. In other words, thought is the cause of it all. If thought is the driving force then that which drives your thoughts determines your actions, and is therefore in the driver's seat of your mind. That which is in the driver's seat of your mind controls you. Who and or what is in the driver's seat of your mind? If man can answer that question then most of his problems can be solved. The enemy within cannot be subdued without confrontation, but confrontation is not physical it is mental. There are nine factors that I use in the Sphere of Thought: 1. **THOUGHT**, 2. **REASON**, 3. **BELIEF**, 4. **DECISION**, 5. **ACTIONS**, 6. **RESULTS**, 7. **INFORMATION**, 8. **CIRCUMSTANCES. THOUGHT** is usually the Reason. The **REASON** is what formulates Belief. **BELIEF** is why we make Decisions. **DECISIONS** drive Actions. **ACTIONS** bring Results. RESULTS produce Information. **INFORMATION** create Circumstances. **CIRCUMSTANCES** drives Thought. Those nine factors, when studied and understood can help you subdue the enemy within without a physical confrontation. It places you in the driver's seat of your mind and in control of the one factor that makes the 9th factor, and unifies the 8 factors: **CHOICE!** Gain control of the 9 factors and you can control Cause. Those who control CAUSE produce **EFFECT. "THE SUPREME ART OF WAR IS TO SUBDUE THE ENEMY WITHIN".**

"THE STRUGGLE CONTINUES" M. Djhuiti Menes

WORD 44

"TROY DAVIS"

Troy Davis is a prisoner on death row in the Georgia State Prison. He is schedule to be killed on September 21, 2011 at 4:00 p.m. Eastern Standard Time in Jackson, Georgia. He was convicted of killing an off duty police officer. Seven of the nine witnesses who testified against him have recanted their statements. They were pressed and coerced by police, to lie and testify to fabricated evidence. Now, some of the witnesses who are coming forward about Troy Davis innocence are being threatened and attack. Before his death, Troy Davis will get to spend six hours with his family. He refused a last meal. Troy said that no matter what happened to him, we all should fight to end the death penalty. I am against the Death Penalty. It is trivial to argue whether or not the death penalty is a just penalty. Those of us who have had a taste of how unjust this criminal justice system is know that in an unjust system any conviction is out of order. For anyone to receive the death penalty in an unjust system is state sponsored murder. But what is even more unjust, is after being trapped off in a system that we know to be unjust based on what we have experienced; we continue to prey on each other. With all that we know, with all that we have been through, we still don't seem to understand that one convict is all convicts, in the sense that we are all citizens of a prison living in cities called a penal institution. Our problems are one, so our aims, our goals, and our destiny should be one: **JUSTICE AND EQUITY FOR ALL CONVICTS.** Therefore, we are all **TROY ANTHONY DAVIS.** An injustice done to one convict is an injustice done to all convicts. **STRUGGLE & UNITY.**

"THE STRUGGLE CONTINUES" M. Djhuiti Menes

WORD 45

"THEY AIN'T PLAYING FAIR"

They break the law to enforce the law. They plant and fabricate evidence against us just to hold us captive in a cave called jail. They round up a group of performers who are willing to sellout for a few scraps, a dollar and or the illusion of freedom. Some performers/clowns will sell their grandmother out. They put on a staged play called a trial, knowing that the verdict will be guilty because they wrote the script and paid the actors. They ignore any written laws that are favorable to us. When we catch them in a lie, they say it was a harmless error. They keep us in prison for life or for long periods of time on a technicality. They put innocent men and women to death for wicked and political reasons just like they did when they murdered Troy Davis. They saw Troy just like they see all of us, as slaves who have no rights. When they killed Troy, they killed all of us. Some of us realize it. Some of us don't know, and some of us don't care. They have destroyed our minds. The proof that they have destroyed our minds is the fact that we have accepted and participate in their modern day slave racket. They use the 13th Amendment to justify their actions. **ALL CONVICTS ARE CONSIDERED SLAVES.** Some of realize it, some of us don't know, and some of us don't care. They condition us to hate ourselves, to prey and snitch on each other. They use the weak up. Then throw them back to the wolves. They rob and cheat us and the weapon they use is our ignorance. They run a monopoly and we buy the scheme because we bow down to our carnal desires; sight, taste, touch, smell and hearing. And we wonder why; **THEY AIN'T PLAYIN FAIR.**

"THE STRUGGLE CONTINUES" M. *Djhuiti Menes*

WORD 46

"IDLE TALK & GOSSIP"

If the words we speak are the thoughts of our heart, and if

an idle mind is the devils work shop; when we participate in

IDLE TALK we are speaking with hardened hearts (crooked

minds) that is a haven for wickedness and bad deeds. When

we **GOSSIP** for recreation with the intent to slander we are

wasting our time, and therefore, time waste us. Waste is

something that is useless, worthless, and has no real value.

If we can tell a tree by the fruit it bears, we can see the true

worth of a person, not by what comes out of their mouths, but

by what is manifested through their actions. "But it is better to

be thought of as a fool than to open your mouth and remove

all doubt". **IDLE TALK** is often symbolic of a cluttered brain

that confuses correct with incorrect. People who are loud

mouths, for the most part, are nothing more than braying

asses or barking dogs, they make loud sounds but they're not

saying anything worth listening to. However, there are some

loud people who seek to bring joy to the hearts of men by

making us all laugh. Those people are the creator's gift to us

all because a good laugh can save a life. But **IDLE TALK &**
GOSSIP is a poor form of communication, entertainment and
amusement that should not be taken serious. Most rappers
use **IDLE TALK & GOSSIP** to make money: If a rapper in a
video says, "They charged me with the **RICO ACT.** I faced
the needle but they gave me life because I wouldn't tell them
where **RICO AT.**" It ain't real talk, it's **IDLE TALK & GOSSIP**
for sell to all who will buy it. If you buy that **BS** you could be
buying a ticket back to prison, which is the reason why a lot of
us came back, we bought the **BS: IDLE TALK & GOSSIP.**

"THE STRUGGLE CONTINUES" M. Djhuiti Menes

WORD 47

"PSYCHOLOGICAL WARFARE"

The science of directing the mind and behavior by way of schemes implemented to weaken or destroy an individual or group. Psychological Warfare is a weapon of mass destruction used by our oppressor to create conditions that is ideal for them to continue to oppress us. The oppressor releases a host/ virus (lies, trickery, deception, false images, and unreachable concepts and almost impossible ideals) that attacks the mind. This virus is usually in the form of information or propaganda designed to stimulate the brain, which moves the body into action. It is the cause that produces the effect. Once we are infected, we become puppets on a string chasing a dream. The reality we seek, either does not exist or cannot be reached from the station we currently occupy in life; especially for those of us who are ignorant. Yet we still use the product that was distributed to us by the manufacturer of deception. This product has proved to be detrimental to all of us and that is why some of us are in prison. If a company sells you a product that doesn't work the way they say it works you can charge

113

INSIDE THE INSIDES MIND

that company with false advertisement. And if their product harms us we can sue the company. But when we are tricked and or deceived, we claim responsibility for the effect without questioning the cause that produced the effect. I hope I didn't go to deep with explaining the concept of **PSYCHOLOGICAL WARFARE** to help us better understand who we are, what we're dealing with and how we got here. No conscious convict is an enemy to another convict. We are brothers in the Struggle for liberation. "The greatest weapon in the hands of the oppressor is the mind of the oppressed", **MLK.**

"THE STRUGGLE CONTINUES" M. Djhuiti Menes

WORD 48

"WHO ARE YOU?"

Why do you exist? Do you function with reason? What is your purpose? In the book, As A Man Thinketh by James Allen, on page fifteen, he said, "man can find every truth connected with his being, if he will dig deep into the mine of his soul...." Who are you? That is a question that we are constantly answering by what we do, which is a manifestation of what we think. We exist to serve, but how and who we serve is depended upon our frame of reference, that is, the ideas that we have accepted as truth. Reason is the proper exercise of the mind. A wasted mind can't reason; it functions without reason, and our minds are being wasted when we do things that are unreasonable. Through experience we can find our purpose, but only through feeding the mind correct knowledge will we learn how to fulfill our purpose. However; knowing, and having the ability to do, are two separate things. We know a lot but do very little, especially when it comes to laws that are unjust. We are quick to address the injustices that we do to each other which is nothing compared to the injustices that is done to us by the powers that be; who are MEGATRONS, that breed DECEPTIVE-CONS, that mix among and deceives the so called CONS. But if you're Optimistic and Primed you peeped the GAME, so when Sentinel gave his spill Optimistic Prime new it was LAME; He left Megatron SPINELESS and Sentinel TIMELESS. Optimistic Prime stayed true and didn't TRADE, transformed but did not FADE; New his purpose and refuse to be PLAYED, by deceptive-cons still in the first GRADE. Now look in the mirror and ask: WHO ARE YOU?

"THE STRUGGLE CONTINUES" M. Djhuiti Menes

WORD 49

"REALISM"

What is it? **REALISM** is undisputed facts based on what can be proven. Realism is not based on Theories, Opinions, Assumptions or Beliefs. Believing something does not mean it is true. Belief and Truth have two separate meanings. Some of us would like to believe that we're in a **CAR.**

[Note: A CAR is a prison gang, a group of men from a particular geographical location, and or a group, usually more than 10 that hang together.]

In **REALISM**; "a **CAR** is a vehicle that has many parts working together to perform a function that is beneficial to its passengers, taking them to and from their destinations". Using the term Realism, we can argue that there are not many **CARS** in fact, just parts that have the potential to become **CARS.** If we use the term Belief, we can say that there are numerous cars. In **REALISM**; when the parts of a **CAR** are only working together when it's time to crash the **CAR**, it is not a **CAR**, it is a convenient tool for destruction? We are the sum total of our experiences. What we have become is a direct result of what we have accepted as truth. But what we have accepted as truth may not be truth. Believing something does not mean it is the truth. However, I am not suggesting that a person should denounce their Beliefs; the intelligent thing to do is to make your belief work in the best interest of each part of the **CAR.** Then the parts will become a **CAR** in Reality; going somewhere! Never stagnate! But a **CAR** that is wrecked is at a standstill and cannot be driven. The broken parts of the wrecked **CAR** must be fixed and working together if the **CAR** is to be driven. Some cars are tight and some cars need to be put in the shop. We definitely need more Mechanics around here. That's **REALISM!**

"THE STRUGGLE CONTINUES" M. Djhuiti Menes

WORD 50

"REVOLVING DOOR"

A REVOLVING DOOR is the door that most people who keep coming in and out of prison use. Some people come back to prison so much that you would think they like it here. But that is not the case. One of the reason people come back to prison is because they have empty tool bags or tool bags with very little tools in them. An empty tool bag is symbolic of a person with little or no education and few social skills. This problem can be corrected, but the person who keeps coming back to prison has to first accept the fact that they have a problem, and that coming back and forth to prison is not normal or sane behavior. Unfortunately, most recidivist (people who come back and forth to prison) think they have all the answers, and therefore, you can't tell them anything. So when they come back to prison they do the same things that they did before they left. They don't realize that one of the definitions of insanity is **"TO REPEAT THE SAME BEHAVIOR AND EXPECT DIFFERENT RESULTS"**. Only when they can be taught something will they be able to get out of prison and stay out. So the only thing that you can say to hard heads (young and old) who don't want to learn and listen to reason, is, "I See You When You Get Back". I know that sounds kind of harsh, but some of us need shock therapy for a point to get across to us. Some of us are just hard headed and stiff neck zombies. And what is scary is that those of us who have children can teach them that coming back and forth to prison is cool; because our children often judge us by what we do. Isn't that the very reason why some of us are here? Some of us were those children who were taught that prison is cool.

"THE STRUGGLE CONTINUES" M. Djhuiti Menes

WORD 51

"SOMETHING TO PROVE"

One of the most dangerous types of people in the world is people with **SOMETHING TO PROVE**. And what makes them even more dangerous is when they don't know what it is they're trying to prove or who it is they're trying to prove it to. Two main characteristics of people with **SOMETHING TO PROVE** is **INSECURITY & IGNORANCE**. People who are insecure and suffer from a loss of self worth try to compensate for that loss by committing extremely foolish acts. These acts seem perfectly normal to those with **SOMETHING TO PROVE** because their foolishness is often an accepted part of their behavior to their peers. Take for instance a person who will die over a table, a remote control, a television, a cell, a spot and or a location. I use to think that this was normal behavior until my sister gave me a reality check. Her exact words were, "Brother you're a damn fool if you are willing to die or hurt someone over some government property that you don't own. They put that sh#$ there before you got there and it's gonna be there when you leave. Furthermore, they put your ass there, and Mamma ain't gonna understand or wanna here that sh#$ if you get caught up..." I needed to hear that. People who love you and care about you will tell you like it is whether you like it or not. But the ignorant man will not take heed. In the book, **THE OLDEST BOOK IN THE WORLD..., THE WISDOM OF PTAH-HOTEP**, it is written that; "An ignorant man is so blind that he takes understanding for ignorance and his own ignorance for the ultimate knowledge". If We Think We Can Save Ourselves.

"THE STRUGGLE CONTINUES" M. *Djhuiti Menes*

WORD 52

"HIDDEN AGENDA"

A **HIDDEN AGENDA** is a plan, a scheme, a purpose and or an idea that is kept secret with the intent to deceive an individual or group into believing the deceiver is trying to accomplish one thing, when the deceiver is actually trying to accomplish something different. In other words, a person with a **HIDDEN AGENDA** is Perpetrating the Fraud. People with **HIDDEN AGENDAS** think they're wise because they have the ability to fool people. They may be slick or wicked, but they are not wise because true wisdom never seeks to deceive or fool anyone. And wisdom is the friend of time because time is usually the one factor that outsmarts people with **HIDDEN AGENDAS**. Time exposes people who perpetrate the Fraud. Time reveals their plans, time teaches us how to read the schemes being run by those with **HIDDEN AGENDAS**. Time affords us the opportunity to learn the deceivers real purpose, and time gives us the skills we need to survive. Ya Dig!

When people with **HIDDEN AGENDAS** are exposed we have the opportunity to disassociate with them. But when we refuse to disassociate with the people we know have **HIDDEN AGENDAS** we become a part of the Fraud. Just like those in society who acknowledge the many Frauds being played on them by the power structure through **HIDDEN AGENDAS** but do nothing about it. Their failure to act makes them a part of the Fraud. It is one thing to be ignorant about the fact that someone is running a **HIDDEN AGENDA** (BOSS GAME) on you, but when you know and do nothing, you're either scared straight or a damned fool.

"THE STRUGGLE CONTINUES" M. Djhuiti Menes

WORD 53

MIS-EDUCATION PART 1

To understand what it means to be mis-educated we have to break down the word mis-education. Mis; is a prefix that means bad: wrong. The root word to education is educe; which means "to bring out"; something latent and or that which is already in you. We are all born with goodness, and this goodness is considered our higher self. We also have a lower self. Mis-education feeds the lower self and education feeds (brings out) the higher self. There are Scientist, Psychologist, Sociologist, Psychiatrist, Mathematician and Scholars of all kinds deciding what should be brought out of us: educed. To do that they carefully plan, strategize and control the information (input) that goes into our minds, and by controlling what goes into our minds they can dictate (output) our actions. When we were born we didn't decide what our addictions, vices, prejudices, problems or bad habits would be. Those who controlled and control the flow of information that we have accepted and accept as truth, made and continue to make those decisions for us. We are all plugged into the Matrix and the Matrix is full of mis-information. What is the Matrix? The Matrix is a systematic network of interconnecting parts that is designed to perform specified task that includes spreading mis-information. Unless we become unplugged, we remain trapped in the Matrix and live our lives as programmed Robots or Puppets under the complete control of puppet masters. How do we unplugged from the Matrix? Read **MIS-EDUCATION PART 2, UNPLUG FROM THE MATRIX.**

"THE STRUGGLE CONTINUES" M. Djhuiti Menes

WORD 54

MIS-EDUCATION PART 2: UNPLUG FROM THE MATRIX

An important method of fighting mis-education is building our Mental Immune System (MSI). We build the MSI by studying and analyzing the root cause of everything. But that will not be enough to **UNPLUG FROM THE MATRIX.** We have to read information designed to wake us up that challenges our thought process. Read books like, "BEHOLD A PALE HORSE" by William Cooper, and "Immaculate Deception" by Russell Bowen. Both books expose some of the wicked criminal acts committed by rulers of this world and the governments they control. For example, in the book, "BEHOLD A PALE HORSE", it explains what happens to prisoners (us) if a war breaks out on American soil. When our **MSI** is strengthened we start to see the Hidden Subliminal messages in objects and Visual Expressions. We begin to understand how sound affects relates to cause and effect. In the television show THE WALKING DEAD, the zombies represent the masses of the people who are unconscious and oblivious to what's going on. If you study history you can easily see how the television show, SONS OF ANARCHY represents a modern day version of an organized group called SONS OF LIBERTY that was first formed in 1765 to fight against high taxes and other laws that were being forced on Americans by the King and Parliament who controlled the colonies. But that control came to an end in 1774 when the FIRST CONTINENTAL CONGRESS adopted the Declaration of Rights and Grievances. If you study/read you can SEE and suppress mis-education, and embrace education. Then you will begin to **UNPLUG FROM THE MATRIX.**

"THE STRUGGLE CONTINUES" M. Djhuiti Menes

WORD 55

"THE VOICE OF REASON"

If you enter a fight without the tools you need to win, more than likely you will lose. Don't let that be the REASON. If you step on the playing field and don't know the rules of the game, more than likely you will lose. Don't let that be the REASON. When you make decisions without thinking you will end up in bad situations, especially when those decisions are impulsive reactions based on emotions. Don't let that be the REASON. We often make excuses as oppose to making adjustments, and as a result, we stagnated our progress; then blame others because we refuse to man up. Don't let that be the REASON. When a wise man gives us advice and we don't take it we often crash. Then, when that same wise man rebukes us for not listening, we hate on him because of the mistakes we made or the bad predicaments we find ourselves in. Don't let that be the REASON. Some of us can't read or write simply because we refuse to learn, then we get upset when a lawyer throw us under the bus or when a policy is being used against us. We start making stupid comments and negative remarks, not based on the facts, but based on opinions, assumptions and speculations. Don't let that be the REASON. Reason is being rational, but when a mind is disturbed it's hard to REASON. However, a disturbed mind need REASON the most because it is easily influenced and vulnerable to Dragon Breath, i.e., negative people with nothing good to say because they have no sense of REASON. We need to start listening to and heeding the advice of "THE VOICE OF REASON".

"THE STRUGGLE CONTINUES" M. Djhuiti Menes

WORD 56

"DEAR MOTHER"

Dear Mother;

I couldn't reach out or express myself to you with an undeveloped mind. Yesterday I knew I knew; I was blind. A day later I thought I knew; I was naive. Today I realize I didn't know what I knew I knew yesterday. And it wasn't until tomorrow that began to understand. Sometimes the circumstances that life places us in are beyond our control and the choices we make as a result of those circumstances are usually made based on our mental capacity, or how much we know. When a man is ignorant his choices are limited. As he matures, his intellectual capacity begins to expand, so does his choices. His ignorance begins to fade and it no longer blinds him. Once the burden of his ignorance is lifted, he is free from the mental and spiritual shackles that held him captive. Physically, I am in prison, but I am mentally and spiritually free. I need you to understand that I am not the person I was yesterday. But yesterday was necessary for me to develop into the man I am today. I am living constructively

131

in the present. Living a constructive life requires a great deal of effort, because there is always obstacles in your path that has to be overcome. One of those obstacles is wanting things that I don't need and neglecting my needs for those wants. It is taking a great deal of discipline to overcome that obstacle but I am winning that battle. I know that I did many things to upset you, and I know that you're tired of hearing apology after apology. But this time I am going to apologize with my actions. I now know that words are good but actions are Supreme. In other words, it has always been in the act and not in the talk.

"THE STRUGGLE CONTINUES" M. Djhuiti Menes

WORD 57

"DEAR FATHER"

I know you're upset with me and think I'm hard headed for not listening to you. Maybe you're a Father who has never been there for me and now you're feeling bad about it. No matter the case, I want you to know that I have managed to make the transition into manhood. All that I have experienced in life help me cope with difficult circumstances and trying times. There have been times when my back was up against the wall and I just didn't know which way to turn, or what to do. And when I needed you the most, you wasn't there. But somehow and some way, I made it through. I can't lie to you Father, it's been rough, and life sure ain't know walk in the park. But with Each Struggle I Grow Stronger. They say pressure breaks pipes, but it also makes diamonds. Father, our foe will never break me, but it has often misdirected me and put me in bad situations. And I may not be the best diamond, but I am among those who stands out in the cluster, shining when it matters most. You would be proud of me Father. In the book, "The Mind of the Soul, Responsible Choice" by Gary

Zukav and Linda Frances they wrote that: "Choice equals Creation. Each choice you make creates experiences for you and others. Your experiences are dramatically and intimately connected to your choices. In fact, the way you perceive yourself is a choice". I often wonder what would it be like if I could sit down and talk to you face to face every day. Then I realized that you have always been here. Within my genetic makeup you exist, and without you there would be no me.

"THE STRUGGLE CONTINUES" M. Djhuiti Menes

WORD 58

"DEAR FAMILY/FRIEND"

Dear Family/Friend,

I know we see the world from a different point of view. I can't judge you based on the way you see things because you are looking at life from the perspective of your experiences, i.e., what you know. We can only go and think as far as our knowledge will allow us. In other words, our mental capacity places limits on us. I won't try to force you to accept a reality that you can't see or comprehend. I would love for you to be able to see the world through my eyes. Unless you have my experiences that will probably never happen. I now know that Knowledge is a gradual process and must be offered in stages just as an infant can't be fed solid food. Don't prejudge me because of the way I see things. I know I can sometimes say things that seem farfetched or outrageous, but I speak from what I have experienced based on what I know, and not based on what I believe or think. When you experience something and learn from that experience, although you may think about and believe in the lesson you've learned, you can also say with certainty that you know it. When knowledge speaks it's usually speaking from experience. I am asking you to focus on the lessons that life has taught me, as opposed to just assuming that I am some kind of radical or out of touch individual. And before you prejudge me, ask yourself two questions; What does he mean by what he is saying? And 2, what is the intent behind his actions? In asking those questions you'll discover who I am, and hopefully, begin to learn about and truly appreciate my evolution. To learn more about yourself, ask yourself those same two questions.

"THE STRUGGLE CONTINUES" M. Djhuiti Menes

WORD 59

"STAY IN YOUR OWN LANE"

Each society provides every person within it a role to play. Some of us are capable of playing more than one role but it's better to be good at one thing then to be bad at many. When we focus on doing what we do best we accomplish more. However, when we play the game of monkey see monkey do, and start trying to duplicate the acts of others we end up appearing as clowns in a circus. What's crazy is that, we are usually the only one who can't see ourselves for the clowns that we have become. But everybody plays the fool sometimes, no exceptions to the rule. Recognizing it is the challenge. If you're good at something, focus on being the best that you can be at it. On the other hand, if you don't think you're good at anything, you should try to spend more time studying yourself. When we study self we discover talents that we didn't know we had, we also have a chance to look at our own flaws and correct what we may not like about ourselves. We would be wise to always look at the man in the mirror, it helps us put things in their proper perspective and find our purpose in life. We cannot find our purpose in life by trying to be like others, in the since that we lose ourselves in another man's reality. That is not to say that we shouldn't try to learn from the positive attitudes and good characters around us, because we should but should stay clear of negative attitudes and bad characters because those mind sets are contagious and stagnate growth and development. We are all gifted in one way or another, find your gift. Recognize the gifts of others and allow all of your gifts to bear fruit by understanding the importance of STAYING IN YOUR OWN LANE.

"THE STRUGGLE CONTINUES" M. Djhuiti Menes

WORD 60

"WHAT'S MINES AIN'T ALWAYS YOURS"

Sometimes it is best to govern only what belongs to you, but we often stick our noses into other people business without sound reason, just cause, or good intentions. When we mind other people business we upset the balance in our own lives, because we put energy into things that we have no true control over, and in the process we lose control of ourselves. Once we lose control of ourselves we defy one of the laws of nature: SELF PRESERVATION. We get lost in a reality that don't exist when we misguide our thoughts and focus on things that are insignificant. Misguided thoughts are dangerous. Misguided thoughts directed at another person is like taking steps into a mind-field, before you know it, you'll find yourself standing in the middle of a contaminated Island that you created through the use of misguided thoughts and wasted energy. And when we attempt to govern what is not ours we are often met with rejection. Most of us can't stand being rejected so we step up the hate game to compensate for our bruised ego. But if we mind our own business and govern that which only belongs to us we won't suffer the shame, self pity, and rejection that comes with worrying about what doesn't concern us. It starts with looking at self. People who feel that they have no self worth refuse to look at self because looking at self forces us to take responsibility for the wars going on inside of our own minds. It's the battle with self that we refuse to fight. Once we defeat the enemy within we'll begin the process of developing our minds, then we can begin to govern ourselves. And being able to govern self is very important because "WHAT'S MINES AIN'T ALWAYS YOURS".

The Struggle Continues". M. Djhuiti Menes. INSIDE THE INSIDES MIND,
dedicated to my Mother Cecelia McEachin.

WORD 61

"CHARGE IT TO THE GAME"

They say that the game is to be sold and the not to be told".
It is truth in that statement because we all pay a heavy price
for not knowing when game is being ran on us. We don't
know a person if we haven't had a chance to observe their
behavior patterns over an extended period of time. And when
you involve yourself in any activity, and don't know every
possible scenario or outcome that could take place as result of
what you're involved in; you really don't know what you're
doing. There is usually several ways you can pay for game,
but I will only outline a couple: 1. You can pay for it through
you own experiences, which is usually the best teacher, but
is full of hard trials because you will no doubt bump your
head on more than one occasion, or you might lose your life.
Like Momma use to say, " a hard head makes a soft ass"; 2.
You can learn from those who know and benefit from their
experiences by listening, and practicing patience and humility,
then applying what you've learned to your walk in life. That
is usually the best path, one that very few of us followed.

There are no short cuts in life, and those looking for short cuts will usually cheat to reach their destination. If you have been cheated by someone trying to take short cuts, it could have been because you was trying to take short cuts yourself. The person that cheated you only beat you to the place where you both were headed: shame. It doesn't matter if you were beat for .25 cents or $2500.00. Some of us even get beat out of years of our lives. It was the price we paid for not allowing the experience of others to teach us the rules of the game. The game is to be sold and not to be told. So CHARGE IT TO THE GAME! "THE STRUGGLE CONTINUES".

M. Djhuiti Menes. INSIDE THE INSIDES MIND,

Dedicated to Cecelia McEachin.

WORD 62

"TRAYVON MARTIN"

Trayvon Martin was the 17 year old child who was lynched in early March 2012 by a 28 year neighborhood watchman named George Zimmerman. Zimmerman admitted that he killed Trayvon. Now Trayvon's family and millions of Americans are screaming for justice. They want Zimmerman arrested. The arrest of Zimmerman would not mean justice for Trayvon because Trayvon represents more than just one person. TRAYVON MARTIN represents all who have suffered and continue to suffer from the onslaught of this oppressive regime called the United States of {Incorporated} America. Trayvon Martin was tried, convicted and executed without a trial. As was many of us: Trayvon Martin was tried by a mindset that is full of prejudices and hatred for Black people and oppressed people in general. Trayvon Martin was convicted because of the stereotypes and the wicked stigmas that are placed on Black men, and these same stereotypes and stigmas created the tainted mind that killed Trayvon and continues to kill us. Trayvon Martin was executed because the life of a Black Man is seen as worthless in the minds of Racist prejudice bigots with no compassion, no mercy, dead hearts and damned souls. That is the kind of mind that murdered Trayvon Martin. That is the kind of mind that write and pass dangerous laws that target poor people. That is the kind of mind that divide and conquers poor people and have us fighting against our own best interest in the name of race, Geographics, gang and political affiliation. Trayvon Martin didn't deserve to die and neither did TROY DAVIS. Just as many people don't deserve the many injustices that are cleverly orchestrated against us by the rulers of this world. But it ain't what happens to us, it's how we handle it that matters. What are we going to do? Let's stop talking the talk and start walking the walk.

"The Struggle Continues". *M. Djhuiti Menes, INSIDE THE INSIDES MIND,*

dedicated to my Mother Cecelia McEachin.

WORD 63

"RECKLESS DISREGARD"

RECKLESS DISREGARD, as I use it here, means "the invading of a person's personal space without care or concern of how your actions affect that person. RECKLESS DISREGARD is a form of blatant disrespect. The people who practice it are usually unaware of their actions. However, there are some who practice RECKLESS DISREGARD and are totally aware of what they do and how their actions affect others. These people are selfish and inconsiderate; self is their primary concern and they lack empathy and compassion for others. These individuals have tunnel vision, and if you can't teach or reach them, you would be wise to avoid them because they create problems then lay back and watch the manifestation of their evil deeds. If your personal space is invaded by someone exercising RECKLESS DISREGARD, and you choose to address the disrespect, you must keep in mind that you are addressing an ignorant and/or unconscious person. Understanding who and what you're dealing with gives you an edge. In other words, you don't spank or discipline a toddler for not knowing, you nurture it; you feed it right knowledge and right guidance and give it time to grow into understanding. Be mindful that there are some adults with the mind of toddlers, therefore, patience and understanding is one of the keys to dealing with those who practice RECKLESS DISREGARD. Do not argue or even debate with a person who practices RECKLESS DISREGARD. Arguing with a person who practices RECKLESS DISREGARD makes you look stupid. And debating with those who practice RECKLESS DISREGARD, especially when you know that you're dealing with a RECKLESS individual; means that you are being RECKLESS because you are DISREGARDING that which you know. THINK FIRST!

"The Struggle Continues". M. Djhuiti Menes.

WORD 64

"NEVER ACCEPT DEFEAT"

I have watch many individuals bend and break as a result

of not being able to deal with the reality of being in prison.

Some in prison even attempt to commit and commit suicide.

The adversities and hardships of doing time in prison ain't no

joke. Then when you add the prison politics to the equation,

prison life can at times be a living hell. In fact, being in

prison is hell on earth. Hell is defined as, "a place or stated

of misery, torment, or wickedness". I remember how it was

I was in prison. From my experience; if you change your

perception you can change your reality; and that sometimes

take innovative thinking and a great imagination. Notice,

I said, "when I was in prison". I am incarcerated but I am

not in prison. Brother Demond Jackson, the founder of the

M.E.N. S.T.O.P. program often states that, "CHANGING

THE EQUATION CHANGES THE SOLUTION". Let's change

the equation. This is how I see it: I am not a prisoner, I am a

student in the classroom of life and my teacher is everything

in the universe. Although I am physically incarcerated, I refuse to be captured mentally, and I will not put my mind in prison. My mind belongs to me, therefore, I will cultivate it, and plant within it, only seeds that bear good fruit. My Harvest will be less complaining and more actions, finding constructive solutions to what I see as problems by applying what I know to circumstance. I cannot do that from prison, and neither can you. Many have tried and most have failed: ESPECIALLY THOSE WHO DON'T READ. Accepting prison is just like accepting defeat. I can't speak for you, but I will "NEVER ACCEPT DEFEAT".

"The Struggle Continues", M. Djhuiti Menes.

WORD 65

"SEEDS OF DESTRUCTION"

SEEDS OF DESTRUCTION are negative words, images and concepts that enter the mind and develops into a thought. Thoughts that are produced by SEEDS OF DESTRUCTION develops a false perception. How we see a thing or circumstance determines how we deal with it because our perception drives our reality. SEEDS OF DESTRUCTION can make a strong man weak and a weak man kill. SEEDS OF DESTRUCTION distorts reality. Once your reality becomes distorted you lose your sense of reason and you make bad choices. Bad choices turn into bad [acts] deeds, and those deeds are the manifestation of SEEDS OF DESTRUCTION entering into a weak mind. It is symbolic of being bitten by a snake; if you're not immune to the venom, or don't have the cure, you will die. In other words, people who plant SEEDS OF DESTRUCTION are snakes. If you are a tool being used by a snake you are dead. However, if you're immune, the SEEDS OF DESTRUCTION planted by the snake die before they turn into bad acts. If you're not immune, a cure to the poisonous

149

venom is consciousness. To understand consciousness you must understand unconsciousness. Unconsciousness is being sleep, unaware and or naive. Consciousness is being awake, aware and or hip to what's happening. When the snake knows that you're hip to what's happening he understands that biting you is suicide for him, but that still doesn't stop him from looking for fertile soil in which to plant his SEEDS OF DESTRUCTION. THINK!

The Struggle Continues, Master Djhuiti Menes.

WORD 66

"TUG OF WAR"

Most of us are in a constant battle with all of the personalities and characters around us. And in many ways our behavior is influenced by some of those personalities and characters. On top of that, some of us struggle with multiple personalities, character defects and mental disorders: Obsessive-compulsive, Manic Depressive, Bipolar, etc... Trying to balance it all out is like a mental TUG OF WAR. On the one side of the rope {mind} there is SANITY and on the other side of the rope {mind} there is INSANITY. Both are pulling hard to win over your mind. The one you feed the most gains strength, so pay close attention to the things that influence your behavior, particularly the personalities and characters around you because they are either giving strength to SANITY or INSANITY. You can give yourself a mental stability test by monitoring your own behavior patterns over a short or extended period of time to gage where you are mentally. Get a sheet of paper, draw a line down the middle of the paper, on the left side of the paper write insane acts, and on the right side of the paper write sane acts. What you see about yourself as negative, write it on the left side of the paper, what you see about yourself as positive write it on the right side of the paper. Number the acts on each side of the paper and whichever scores the most is winning the TUG OF WAR. It's hard to identify and deal with the things that have a negative effect on the mind. What affects the mind affects the body. Mental poison kill the mind just as other poisons kill the body. Allowing negative thoughts to dictate your behavior is like consuming mental poison. Identify the poison, attack it with your conscience; and you win the TUG OF WAR.

The Struggle Continues, Master Djhuiti Menes.

WORD 67

"BONE CRUSHER"

The word BONE as I use it here, means "slanderous words that are spoken with the intent to disrespect, defame, and or lie on a person with no regard for the truth". The word CRUSHER, as I use it here, means "to expose and examine the characteristics of people who put out bad BONES and drop SEEDS OF DESTRUCTION". People who put out bad BONES are usually Attention Seekers, Salt Shakers, Cowards, Petty, and or Clowns. Every word that a person speaks has intent and purpose behind them. The Attention Seeker is usually a loud mouth that puts on a show and drops bad BONES for the sole purpose of attracting Attention; Ignore them. The Salt Shakers have nothing good to say about anyone or anybody, they drop bad BONES with the intent to plant SEEDS OF DESTRUCTION; Watch out for them. Cowards drop bad BONES out of fear, and when their words come back to hunt them, they manipulate the circumstances and shift the blame; Stay away from them. The Petty is always trying to find a come up, they drop bad BONES to put themselves in a position to be able to use you; Let them know you're hip. Clowns are always trying to get a laugh, and most Clowns don't even realize their own buffoonery, they drop bad BONES and are usually unaware that they have offended someone; Tolerate them. The BONE CRUSHER is wise enough to understand the intent behind the words spoken by knowing the characters that's speaking the words. The BONE CRUSHER is a thinker, he understands that some people will say things without knowing the full impact of their words. Therefore, the BONE CRUSHER uses his mental filter to Ignore, Watch out for, Stay away from, Let' em know he's hip, or Tolerate those who drop bad BONES.

The Struggle Continues. M. Djhuiti Menes.

WORD 68

"RE-DIRECT YOUR THOUGHTS"

The things that we are dedicated to have a lot to do with the way we direct our thoughts. We make progress, or we regress based on the direction of our thoughts which produce action or no action. Some of us think as individuals, and some of us think as a group but are only truly concerned with self. Therefore, we often neglect the best interest of the group to satisfy our own desires, which leaves the group with no real aim, no goal, no purpose or direction. If you're thinking as an individual do you have a goal? If you have a goal what are you doing to accomplish that goal? If you're a part of a group, does that group have an aim, a goal, and a purpose? If your answer is yes, then what is your group doing to accomplish that aim, that goal, and that purpose? Is that aim, that goal, and that purpose in the best interest of the group, and in your best interest as an individual? If you answered yes to that last question, then maybe you're in the right place mentally. If you answered no to the last question then maybe you are not in the right place mentally and you need to RE-DIRECT

YOUR THOUGHTS. Association can often create simulation, and we tend to gravitate toward people of our likeness which says a lot about who we are as individuals and or as a group. "RE-DIRECT YOUR THOUGHTS" means evaluating your circumstances and making sure your circumstances, and or the circumstances of your group, fits your best interest, and or the best interest of your group. Hard Trials are Necessary to Establish Truth; don't be afraid to "RE-DIRECT YOUR THOUGHTS".

WORD 69

"THE WEIGHT OF THE WORLD"

THE WEIGHT OF THE WORLD is symbolic of responsibility. We face many problems in this world. And sometimes the pressure is so heavy that it feels as if THE WEIGHT OF THE WORLD is on our shoulders. Every step we take becomes a struggle. Cowards complain about THE WEIGHT OF THE WORLD and do nothing but talk about the men and women who handle THE WEIGHT OF THE WORLD with care. Strong men and women are not afraid to carry THE WEIGHT OF THE WORLD. However, wise men and women know if we move to fast we could fall and drop THE WEIGHT OF THE WORLD where it doesn't belong. If we move to slow THE WEIGHT OF THE WORLD will wear us down, and then we become no good to ourselves and others. If we don't move at all, it is a sign to the world that we have given up, and THE WEIGHT OF THE WORLD will cave in on us. Therefore, no matter the situation or the circumstance we must move with grace to balance THE WEIGHT OF THE WORLD. The more responsibilities we have the heavier THE WEIGHT OF

THE WORLD becomes. Conscious people understand that with power comes great responsibility. When great power is overcome by emotions we lose our sense of responsibility and our ability to respond effectively. A balanced mind carefully evaluates THE WEIGHT OF THE WORLD and does not succumb to pressure. It remembers the past and thinks for the future. A balanced mind places principles in front of emotions and let wisdom be its guide. A balance mind places reason in front of instinct because instinct functions without a conscience. A balanced mind is not afraid of responsibility. Can you handle it?: "THE WEIGHT OF THE WORLD".

WORD 70

STRUGGLE & UNITY

[FREEDOM OF EXPRESSION]

REAL TALK

An oppressor recognizes that is far more likely for a Black man to rebel in society, so the oppressor goes all out to oppress the Black man on all fronts. [When I use to the term Black Man I am speaking of all men/people that suffer, and has suffered under the iron hand of the oppressor] Conscious Black men are well aware of the schemes that are taking place and we use strategies and put forth true and valid efforts to fight against those schemes. REAL TALK!

MIS-EDUCATION

The mis-education of the young Black children, and all young males and females amounts to the worst kind of child abuse. Many of us were not only mis-educated, we were also false indoctrinated and trained to worship materials things as if they are Gods. This causes us to neglect the spirit within us, and as a result we fail to build the content of our characters. When we worship things that bring us no true salvation we start to desire that which kills us within and destroys us without. And when our desires are not met we/oppressed people begin to attack each other and unconsciously assist in our own destruction. As a direct result of unconscious self destruction, we fail our family, we fail our community, and we ultimately fail ourselves. REAL TALK!

BREAKING THE CODE

We must break the code of the enemy which have us fighting against each other as oppose to fighting for each other. Once we break the code of the enemy we will start the process of healing and loving ourselves. And only then can we love each other and become a true Brotherhood.

Everything we do should have sound reason and purpose because when we function without sound reason and purpose our lives become senseless. We may gain a few cheap frills and thrills living a senseless life; but immediate and instant gratification should never be an option when it interferes with our moral integrity and our long term goals. Especially when it leaves us stuck with the same oppressed minds that keep us stagnated. An intelligent person, particularly a consciously

160

intelligent Black man, will never allow himself to be dumb down or shamed for the purpose of immediate or instant gratification. He has focus and discipline, he can see the whole picture of life and not just one part of THE FRAME... REAL TALK!

LIBERATION

I offer you truth. If you're a person who is about the struggle and liberation for oppressed people and not some Polished fool who talk a good game but disregard wisdom, you are an asset to our people. Keep up the good fight. However, frauds stop progress and they put liberation out of reach. No one respects a fraud, not even the person perpetrating the fraud. Be true to what you say you represent because being real saves lives and offers hope. REAL TALK!

NEVER FOLD

Never bend or fold to oppression. Especially when you are right. Stand on principles. Everyone, even the oppressor, respects people who stand on their principles. You may suffer for standing firm but you will always have the utmost respect for the person you see in the mirror. REAL TALK!

DON'T BE DEFEATED

This society is structured to defeat Black manhood so recognize your opponent. Opposition comes in many forms. It could be as great as the government, or as small as a miserable friend who sometimes function consciously or unconsciously trying the defeat your manhood, i.e., trying to get you to compromise the sound principles on which you stand. When you compromise your principles, that's the beginning of the collapse of your character. Be careful, some people use all kinds of techniques to try to get you to conform to straight up and down BS. Stand firm, don't be defeated, not even by your own ego. The ego is one of the most dangerous enemies. The ego has a mind of its own, so never let it override your sense of reason because it will cause you to crash. REAL TALK!

FRIENDSHIP

A true friend will add to your strength and never let you fall. A true friend will never allow anyone to manipulate you, use you or waste your time. REAL TALK!

MANHOOD

A MAN acts in accordance with what and who he is. Yesterday he was a boy, and before that he was a baby. With

162

each stage of his existence he acts accordingly. A MAN

does all that he can do to enter into a Supreme Mental State.

Manhood is not a given, it must be developed. And there are

many trials and tribulations that males go through to develop

into MANHOOD. Men are careful, strong, positive, and

proactive. Some males never reach MANHOOD. REAL TALK!

THE WAR

In reality we have been at war from the moment we came out

of the womb. We are taught lies from the cradle to the grave in

the form of nursery rhymes and fairy tales. Lies ruin destinies.

Lies and deception breeds ignorance. Our war is not against

each other, it is against ignorance wherever ignorance rears

its ugly head. Ignorance stunts our growth and keeps us from

developing into MANHOOD. We overcome ignorance, we win

the war. REAL TALK!

"DON'T FALL TO FRUSTRATION"

It is natural to become frustrated with some things, but don't

act out of frustration because an act out of frustration is

usually an impulsive act. Impulsive acts are quick avenues

to self destruction and the destruction of others. Know the

difference between being mad and being upset. When you're

mad you're not in your right state of mind. Basically, when you're mad, you could be out of your of mind. But when you're upset your sense of reason is in order and you can still make good decisions. You must know that most of the ignorant things we do is learned behavior. Somebody, and or some entity taught us how to act the way we act, and react the way we react. We must unlearned the things that hinder us.

"HOPELESSNESS"

Never fall into a state of hopelessness. Always know that there is meaning to your life. And never give up on you. REAL TALK!

Peace and Blessings, STRUGGLE & UNITY. May the Universe favor you.

"THE STRUGGLE CONTINUES".

Your Brother and Humble Servant, M. Djhuiti Menes.

WORD 71

"THE MIND"

It is said that, "the greatest weapon in the hands of the oppressor is the mind of the oppressed". That statement is very powerful to those who understand what it means. Once you understand that statement, you can begin to use your weapon [MIND] effectively, and or take your weapon back from those who abuse it. The greatest weapon available to any man is his mind. This weapon has been used to build, and it has been used to destroy. If your mind is in the hands of others, those people can use your mind to their benefit as a weapon to build or destroy, for good or for bad in their best interest. In other words, those we follow guide our thoughts. Those who guide our thoughts are in control of our minds. If they can control your mind they can enslave your will. That is one reason why we must carefully examine the mind of the people in our immediate circle. We must know what their immediate and long term goals are; then we can make a conscious choice to keep them armed with our minds, or disarm them of our minds. For example: When you know someone doesn't have your best interest at heart and you allow them to continue to use your mind; you have lost your mind, and it is damned. Most of us would like to think that we are independent thinkers, but in reality what we think and do is often based on the thought process of others. There is not one being on the Planet whose mind is independent of others; all languages, all alphabets, numerical systems and cultures are formulated in the mind of others and passed down from one generation to the next. Guard your thoughts and control your mind. A NEW DAY!

THE STRUGGLE CONTINUES.

WORD 72

"NO DOUBT"

Doubt is the seed of defeat. Once doubt enters the mind, failure becomes your ideology. Even clear victories will be seemed as a defeat because you doubt your ability to win. Therefore, when you lose a battle you will surrender in the war, because you fail to understand that battles are won and lost in the process of winning wars. When you have NO DOUBT in you, you see defeat as a temporary setback. When there is NO DOUBT in your mind you see defeat as a victory because the experience you gain in what appeared to be a loss was a lesson that you could not have learned any other way. When there is NO DOUBT in your mind, you will challenge an opponent even when the odds are against you, and you win because your opponent never expected you to put up a fight. When you put up a strong fight, using your mind over matter; you will not only gain the respect of your opponents, you will place doubt in their minds. Remember, doubt is the seed of defeat, and once defeat enters the mind, the road ahead leads to failure. Avoid those who doubt themselves because they can pull you into a pit full of failures that will fill your mind with doubt because they chose to drown in shallow graves called envy, fear and ignorance. And they welcome your company. Great minds have NO DOUBT in them. Minds that have NO DOUBT in them never listen to pessimistic people, because pessimistic people stop great ideas from becoming beautiful realities. If you have a goal that you're trying to accomplish and asked me for my advice on where to start; I would say start with NO DOUBT! NO DOUBT!

"The Struggle Continues." Master Djhuiti Menes.

WORD 73

"FIGHTING THE WRONG BATTLE"

There are three things that a Boy has absolutely no control over; his pride, his ego and his tongue. When he fails to control his pride, his ego and his tongue, he often puts on a display of selfish, inconsiderate buffoonery that does harm to him and those associated with him. These children are often boys in men's bodies; they have grown old but have not grown up. To disrespect a person means nothing to them, because they have not been taught how to respect others or themselves, and they are often surrounded by people who condone their foolish behavior. It takes a man to raise a man, and most of these oversized boys have been raised by females; [no disrespect to women intended] that is part of the reason why they are so emotional and throw temper tantrums and want to FIGHT whenever they don't get their way. Most of them want to FIGHT because they have often suffered some mental trauma in the past and they are still hurting as a direct result of that trauma. And hurt people hurt people. If they fail to deal with the psychological trauma they suffered in the past

169

they will always be FIGHTING THE WRONG BATTLE. Men get emotional, but Men control their emotions with sound reasoning. Men get threatened, but Men assess the threats, and will not waste time, energy or resources addressing a threat that will never materialize. At the same time a man can tell the difference between a threat and an agent posing as a threat to get a reaction. Men get disrespected, but they evaluate the mind set and level of consciousness of the person(s) that disrespected them. Women who read this will appreciate it and may accept it for what it is worth. Boys posing as men who read this will not agree because they have not made the needed transition into manhood, and until they do, they will always be "FIGHTING THE WRONG BATTLE"

WORD 74

"IMAGINE"

To Imagine is to have vision and foresight, to have vision and foresight is to see things before they manifest in reality. If you can see things before they manifest in reality you have the vision and the ability to make those things happen. To make those things happen takes more than mere belief; it takes a mind that can IMAGINE and will go to work. IMAGINE if prisoners wake up and recognize that their suffering is far greater than their differences. IMAGINE if prisoners unite and fight for causes that will have a positive impact on the prison population and their families. IMAGINE prisoners fighting against policies and laws that have a negative effect on them and their families. IMAGINE if prisoners identify 5 major issues that affect prisoners and their families and address those issues legally and constructively, within the rules and regulations, in an organized and structured manner to change and or improve on those policies and issues that affect them and their families. IMAGINE if prisoners set aside race, Geographics and prison politics, and start thinking in the best interest of prisoners and their families before they make decisions. IMAGINE if prisoner's first concerns were better food and living conditions, good educational and vocational job training programs, the ABOLISHMENT OF THE 5K.1, and the reinstatement of conjugal visits in the Federal Bureau of Prisons and All state prisons. IMAGINE if prisoners stop fighting each other over petty issues that could be avoided by showing respect, concern and consideration, and using manners towards each other. IMAGINE if prisoners stop worshiping TV's, Tables, Cells and superficial things that can't help them at all as if those things were Gods. IMAGINE, if those of you in society who have love ones in prisons throughout America and the world, step up to the plate and get involved in the struggle. IMAGINE A NEW DAY! Can you see it? It's coming!

THE STRUGGLE CONTINUES

172

WORD 75

"THE HAMMER"

THE HAMMER is symbolic of the Raw Truth. Reality as we know it is out of order. The people that should be honored are shamed, and the people that should be shamed are honored. Some police try to act like convicts, and some inmates try to act like the police. Conscious people who fight for liberation are often seen as trouble makers by the people they fight for. Foolish men with money is honored by the people they oppress. Weak leaders work against the best interest of the people who follow them. A rebel without a cause is like a stray bullet; it has power and force, but no aim and purpose. Experience is the best teacher if you survive and learn from the experience. If you know a problem exist that you can solve, and you do nothing about it; you're either ignorant, a coward, you agree with the problem, and or you created the problem. A fool can hear, but a fool doesn't listen. If power concedes nothing without a fight, those who refuse to fight make a conscious choice to remain powerless. It's OK to forgive, but you should never forget; when you lose your memory you are subject to being destroyed again. Acting without thinking is like believing everything you hear. Hope creates opportunities because it drives your will to fight for something. Change starts with the first step. A resolution not kept is a waste of carbon dioxide. If you can be bought, you cannot be trusted. Time is intelligent; it will tell you the truth if you're patient. Battles are won and lost, but some wars never end. If you can see, and your mind is fertile, you can use this tool for good: THE HAMMER!

THE STRUGGLE CONTINUES

WORD 76

"HOW TO LOVE A WOMAN: PART 1"

Time and space are the only things that sometimes physically separate a man from a woman. But when two minds become one nothing separates a man and his woman. The material world is not a factor when a man's love for his woman is out of this world. Empathetic listening and reasoning are key factors to understanding and nourishing a woman's heart. Some women (not all) suffer from past traumatic experiences, and those experiences can cause them to act abnormal. And that abnormal behavior will often frustrate men who don't understand and can't relate to the abnormality. If a man doesn't understand the symptom, he can't cure (love) her. Men who don't understand react. Men who understand respond. Reactions are impulsive and can create confrontations. Responses are well thought out and reasonable. If, as a result of some past traumatic experiences a woman has become a Manic Depressive and or Obsessive Compulsive, a man must be able to recognize the symptoms, and have the fortitude and presence of mind, as well as the ability to address her ills rather than fighting her or hating her for not being her true self. Real men do not run from a woman in need of love, he navigates the rough waters until her seas are calmed. Once she recognizes your wit, (love for her) she will submit. But not willingly, she will test you to see if you're the man (love) that you're representing to her. Do not place all of your focus on her physical being, focus first and foremost on her mental, spiritual and psychological well- being. A loved and spiritually well nurtured woman represents a man's paradise. And a consciously intelligent mentally groomed man represents a woman's paradise. "LET YOUR MIND BE HER REFUGE: HOW TO LOVE A WOMAN.

WORD 77

"HOW TO LOVE A WOMAN: PART 2"

Some women don't want to be treated like a queen? No matter what you say or do you get a negative response from her? This means that time and circumstances built a brick wall between her and her true self. Any wall that has been built, can be broke down. Analyze every part of the wall, start with the top, which represents the height of her problems. Each brick in the wall must be carefully removed. Look close enough, you can read the writings on the wall and you will see that each brick represent an issue that she isn't aware of or never dealt with. Address one issue at a time, focusing on her and not "you". Be selfless when addressing her issues. Don't just hear her, listen to her. There is a formula to addressing all of her issues. The answers you seek is in the words she speak: Listen! Respond only when asked. The Bricks will fall and "she" will remove the part of herself that is not true. Give your soul to her, she will be receptive; you will see a part of yourself in her. Your heart will morph into one with hers, and you two will be in harmony with each other. The love you give to her should be as solid as a rock, no wavering. A woman is often a reflection of her man and a man is a reflection of his woman. By that I mean; how they treat each other molds their characters for the better or for the worst. True love removes impediments from her spirit and renders her at peace with herself and in peace with her man. A warm feeling will consume her and she will take great care not to hurt her love one because that would be hurting herself. Treat her like a queen and the sincere seeds you plant in her mind will grow into beautiful flowers.

THE STRUGGLE CONTINUES

WORD 78

"COOPERATIVE ECONOMICS"

We have been conditioned to direct our financial resources and or spend our money against our own best interest. How and where we direct our financial resources directly affects our Social Conditions which has a positive or a negative impact on our well-being. There are approximately 1,400 prisoners in any given Penitentiary. Each prisoner spends an average of $100.00 a month in the commissary, which amounts to $140,000.00. Multiply that by 12, and it's $1,680,000.00 a year that prisoners spend in the commissary with no real Social return or benefit. High prices, cheap products and poor service are what prisoners get for the 1.7 million that they spend in ONE Penitentiary a year. If 1,400 prisoners in ONE Penitentiary send $5.00 a month to a prisoners rights organization, that would amount to $7,000.00 a month. Multiply that by 12 and it amounts to $84,000.00 a year, which is less than 5% of what prisoners spend on average a year in the commissary. Not to mention how much prisoners spend using telephones, emails and on foolishness. That 5%, ($84,000.00) a year can be used to hire and Organization and/or a Law Firm to represent prisoner's best interest on 5 or more major issues that plague prisoners. The organization will fight to change the " UNJUST LAWS and PRISON POLICIES" that have a negative impact on prisoners. And the prisoners who fight within the rules and regulations that are unjustly locked down will have legal representation that will fight in their best interest because they will have intelligently direct their resources to their benefit. That will be, without a doubt or contradictions: COOPERATIVE ECONOMICS.

THE STRUGGLE CONTINUES

To: Barak Obama, President of the

United States of America,

White House/Oval Office,

1600 Pennsylvania Ave, NW

Washington, D.C. 20500

Dear Mr. President,

It is understandable that all crime must be brought to justice;

however, when that Judicial Branch does not adhere to the

laws set forth by the Legislative Branch JUSTICE can never

be served no matter the outcome of a criminal case tried in a

court of law.

Therefore, I, Master Djhuiti Menes, am requesting that you

take notice to the criminal prosecutions that has been and is

currently taking place in the United States of America District

Courts throughout America and its Territories, giving special

attention to the FEDERAL SENTENCING GUIDELINE'S 5k1's

application, and how that provision in and of itself amounts to

invidious discrimination, as it permits/allows a disparity in the

sentencing of individuals charged and convicted of identical criminal acts. It also violates and conflicts with the FEDERAL CRIMINAL CODE AND RULES 18 USC 201 (c) (2), which states:

"whoever, directly or indirectly, gives, offers, or promises anything of value to any person, for or because of the testimony under oath or the affirmation given or to be given by such person as a witness upon trial, hearing, or other proceeding, before any court, any committee of either House or both Houses of Congress, or any agency, commission, or officer authorized by the laws of the United States to hear evidence or take testimony, or for or because of such person's absence there from: shall be fine under this title or imprisoned for more than two years, or both".

The Federal Sentencing Guidelines as noted by the United States Supreme Court in Blakely and Cunningham is UNCONSTITUTIONAL, as the Federal Sentencing Guidelines violates the Fifth Amendment of the United States Constitution. In addition, both Blakely and Rule 404 (b) of the Federal Criminal Codes Rules violates the United States Constitution because they both permit criminal allegations, i.e., conduct and unindicted evidence to come before and be heard by a petit jury the was not indicted by a grand jury.

To ask for justice in a criminal justice system that defines justice ambiguously is more dangerous that Russian Roulette. Therefore, with all due respect Mr. President, I am ASKING FOR EQUALITY! Please address this matter and respond in writing, as I am, still a citizen of the United States of America.

Respectfully,

"Master Djhuiti Menes"

"They hate you when you can see them for who they are, they fear you when they can't control you; and they kill you when you call them out."

"Powerful"
Keep fighting dad.
Respectfully, your Son!

"The hunt is on, the traps have been set. Learn the rules. Its not a game!"

To Order Contact
Prisoners Writes Publishing (PWP)
PO Box 5821
Capital Heights, MD 20791

Email: istruggle360@yahoo.com
facebook: Prisoners Writes Publishing

Made in the USA
Charleston, SC
18 June 2015